SHATTERED

DIVORCE DEVOTIONAL JOURNAL

BY
SHARON STEINMAN
AND
DYANN MUNOZ

Shattered
Divorce Devotional Journal
ISBN: 978-1-936314-89-8

Published by Word & Spirit Publishing
P.O. Box 701403
Tulsa, OK 74170

Sharon's photo by Sue Evans
Dyann's photo by Kim French

My life is an example to many, because you have been my strength and protection. That is why I can never stop praising you; I declare your glory all day long.

—Psalm 71:7-8

DEDICATION

TO MY SISTER, PAM,
WHO HAS WALKED EACH STEP WITH ME
AND ALWAYS MAKES ME LAUGH.
—SHARON

TO MY SISTER, SHARON, AND
MY PRECIOUS FRIEND, TAMI.
THESE WOMEN HAVE STRENGTH AND
FAITH THAT MADE ME STRONGER.
—DYANN

CONTENTS

A NOTE TO THE READER

Please understand that within the pages of this book we offer no case studies, no scientific gathering of data, no religious dogma. We only offer the sharing of hurt, anger, frustration, fear, prayers, and hope from two women who saw a need. We have tried to offer healing, wisdom, and scripture-based comfort. If we discovered some practical ideas along the way, we have shared those as well. Whatever we had to draw on, through the collective of our own personal experiences, our pain, and our process—we offer here. We have spoken with many women who have suffered in ways we haven't personally experienced. We blended their voices with our own and have written in one voice as though one woman were speaking, but only to simplify our singular message of hope and healing. It is our profound hope that you recognize the sisterhood we share and that as you read, you will know you are hearing from women who can relate to your anger, disillusionment, and hurt. These are the lessons we learned.

We begin your journey to healing with the specific emotional challenges that we know will strike you hard and fast. We offer supportive scriptures so you can see for yourself how much God loves you and wants to return you to wholeness. We have learned that saying the scriptures aloud will cause your voice and your spirit to proclaim God's truth and his commitment to you.

We hope to encourage you to journal throughout this process. We have included journaling pages because we feel that being able to express your thoughts and feelings is important for your healing and growth. There is something about pouring out your pain on paper that releases you from carrying it with you. On these journaling pages, we have included what we call "nuggets of truth" that we have learned about God, about his love for you, about his promises to you, and his joy in you. There are also suggestions to speed your healing. These are just tips that can draw you a bit outside yourself or reward the woman that is you, God's precious daughter.

We both went back over our journaling to recall what we experienced, with the hope of consoling you. We can't take away the pain. But perhaps we can bring you a bit of comfort. Perhaps we can show you God's love for you, as you may not have seen it before. Perhaps we can give you some hope, soothe your wounded heart, and love you through this awful time.

We found many books that were helpful to us when some of the healing was done. We encourage you to read those as well. Information is power and we long to see you powerful again. What we didn't find was the book you need for the moment you realize your marriage is falling apart, the moment you are served papers, the day of your court hearing, the day you learn he was cheating, or that he chose his addiction over you. We wanted to write a book that spoke to the earliest fear and pain of an impending or active divorce. We shared our intention with other women who had so many touching stories that served to cement our resolve. This book is intended to bridge the gap between the fragmented woman you are right now and the Bible that you so badly need.

In his love,

Sharon & Dyann

SHARON'S STORY

Dyann and I were close friends, even though a five-hour drive separated us. When I heard Dyann's bad news, I, too, was shocked and so saddened for her. Wanting to help take away her pain, I tried to talk to her as Jesus would, encouraging her with scriptures, sending her uplifting messages, and telling her of God's love for her.

Our phone calls would last for hours and hours. I could hear her tears and knew that her heart was broken. The love, support, and comfort I was able to offer Dyann was timeless. Then, two years after her tragedy, she comforted me when my second husband was divorcing me. When we look back and tell our stories, we are amazed by what God has done for us two broken-hearted women.

I had no idea I was headed for such an emotionally difficult time. It brought new challenges that seemed daunting to me. I had to slug through legal documents and divorce laws for my state. I needed to find a place to live. I needed to figure out a source of income. I needed to break the news to my family and friends. I needed to adjust to being alone. I needed to pick myself up and try to take the next step.

Not only did I have to do the practical day-to-day things to take care of myself, but I had to do it while hounded by fear, hurting at my core, and feeling intensely fragile and completely shattered.

My ex-husband remarried very quickly. I felt like a dirty diaper he had happily tossed in the trash. Now he and his new wife were in the beautiful home we had built together and living the life I once had. The sense of abandonment and rejection brought about intense feelings of fear, loneliness, anger, and resentment, not to mention a devaluing of my self-worth.

I was angry at my ex for all the obvious reasons. I wasn't just mad, I was stewing with anger—so much so that I wanted to set his few hairs on fire. Believe me, I spent a good bit of time on my knees asking God to let me enjoy this image of my ex in flames!

Of course, God did not let me follow through on that impulse. Instead, I had absolute proof God answers prayer and while I was certain of God's love, I often wondered why God didn't save my marriage. I asked him over and over, "Why . . . why did my marriage fail?" My desire to hold my marriage together made its failure that much more painful.

The pain in my heart was so intense that I thought it would kill me. I believed my broken heart would be the end of me. But this was not my end . . . it was my new beginning. God had his healing hand on me even though my swollen, puffy eyes could not see the bright future ahead. I saw a hint of the promise of that future the day I left the courtroom. I was still confused and had many unanswered questions. The future was still unknown. But as I stepped out of the cold, gray courtroom there was a magnificent rainbow arching itself over the courthouse.

My hurting friend, God has a rainbow for you. Dyann and I are sharing our stories and lessons learned so you can see how God healed us and how he wants to heal you. The pain you are suffering today is temporary. There is healing in these pages. The healing doesn't come from our words—but from God.

DYANN'S STORY

My personal experience includes a divorce of my choosing from one man and the death of another man whom I loved dearly. So my perspective is quite different from Sharon's. My divorce happened more than 30 years ago and was the result of my own emotional fragility and collapse. At that time, divorce wasn't very common in my sphere of influence. I was the only divorced person I knew. If there was help or resources available to me then, I didn't know it. I was very naive and an emotional mess. Eventually, my life became manageable, but I never really healed properly.

Most of my pain was self-inflicted. I was married at the tender age of nineteen. I wasn't ready to be a grown woman on my own, much less a wife. Throw in the Vietnam War, a soldier husband, a new baby, living with family, then college life, another baby, and multiple moves—and you could say we had our challenges. I was young, foolish, and deeply flawed. My husband played no part in my crumbling of self—I couldn't have managed a marriage to anyone. I was the inflictor of pain. I was broken and needed fixing, but I didn't have God in my life. I chose divorce, not knowing what else to do. In the end, I only made my mess worse. And it would be years before I faced any of my guilt, resentment, anger, and my inability to forgive myself or anyone else.

Frankly my healing was unfinished when I found love again. But until everything went very wrong, my life was happy. Then my hopeful life took a dramatic turn in the blink of an eye. In that blink, I found myself shattered. I actually felt the sensation of my heart breaking. It felt like the crushing and cracking of my physical heart. It overwhelmed me. And it didn't break once, but over and over again—every time I awoke to a new day. I wasn't having a nightmarish dream. I was living a daily, awful, dark reality that was my new life. Gone were my happy life and my joy.

That relationship never resulted in marriage. With family tragedies, start-up businesses, illness, surgeries, and the deaths of loved ones, there always seemed to be something that made for bad timing for a wedding. Finally, one July we were ready. We took a trip to the Bahamas to plan our destination wedding and buy my wedding ring. We set the date for January.

Over the years we had gone through a great deal. Some of it was pretty awful and some was wonderful beyond my wildest dreams. Now here I was, soon to be married to the man I absolutely adored. Anticipating my wedding day left me almost giddy. But suddenly one December morning, he suffered a fatal heart attack!

I was out of state visiting family. We were chatting excitedly about plans for the upcoming holiday and when I would be home to spend Christmas with my sweetheart. Then the awful call came from his daughter. I could hear the pain in her voice, but I couldn't process what she was saying. I could feel the life drain from my face, down my body, and leave my legs. The world collapsed around me, but I didn't feel pain—not yet. I couldn't feel much of anything except for a sensation of being disconnected. I was numb, like my heart had left me.

Soon after that terrible phone call, the realization of what had happened flooded my being. My sister and her husband consoled me. I couldn't take it all in but I remember them saying, "we can't believe he is dead." *Dead.* The word hung in the air, sort of quivering as though it needed to attach itself to someone. I wanted to brush it away like an annoying insect buzzing near my ear. I remember trying to reason through what was happening. I seemed to be in an echoing fog. I was seeing myself crumble under the weight of the enormous news that my wonderful love was dead. Yearn as I did, I realized I would never be his bride.

A new and intense wave of shock hit me full-force at the airport. I remember very little of that trip home, but I do remember concerned people pawing me, urging me to tell them what was wrong. Was I sure I wanted to board the plane? Did I need a doctor? Was I in pain? My God, it was the worst pain I'd ever experienced in my life. My lungs burned with the effort to breathe. I wanted desperately for the crushing pain in my chest to subside. I feared my heart was cracking into pieces. I was so emotionally fragmented that I could hardly get myself from one plane to the other. I was lost in a sea of travelers. I wanted to scream at the agony of my loss. I wanted to hit something, to lash out in some way. I thought I would explode from the combustion brewing and building deep inside me.

Somehow I managed to get home. Someone met me at the airport, but I couldn't tell you who. I am certain they must have tried to console me, but I don't recall the words. Once back at my home, I know people came to hug me, to pray with me, and just be there. But I couldn't say who they were either. I was so deep in the black hole of my loss, I couldn't take in anything around me. I hope I consoled his sweet daughter and adoring mother, but I don't know if I did.

The day of the funeral was an equal blur, cloaked in a muffled fog. I was struggling to understand and accept that he was gone. I do remember writing him a love letter and tucking it in his shirt. It was important to me that my love be laid to rest with my words close to his heart. I also remember kissing him again and again and again in his casket. I remember telling myself to back away so others could pay their respects but I couldn't. I tried. I really tried, but I just couldn't. In mere moments they would close his casket and I could never see or kiss him again. It was unbearable.

I'd known pain in my life, both physical and emotional. But never had I known such a loss. I had placed so much hope in our future. I wanted his kids and grandkids and my kids and grandkids to be truly "ours." I felt so much love for this man, I couldn't think past the crush of regret and loss. I didn't believe I could survive without him. I didn't want to live with such an overwhelming void. All I had to fill that void was anger, hurt, confusion, regret, uncertainty, and pain.

When the numbness began to subside and the full measure of pain could be realized, it was bad—really bad. The overwhelming feeling was anger. I had prayed for this man and our life together for so many years. I thought God was finally listening. Now this? My anger at God was thunderous. I remember balling up my fist in a menacing gesture aimed at the heavens. I believe I might have taken a swing at God, if I'd had the chance. I'd clung to the belief that God wanted this marriage for me, for us. I shudder now, to think how I threatened God. I told him I would never trust him again. I told him he was unkind and unjust. Yet at the same time, I cried out to God to save me from this pain.

I went through months unable to accept sympathy, compassion, joy, or love from those who cared about me. I was in such a gray place, it angered me to see the sun shining. I wanted the world to look as gray and miserable as I felt. But dear, wonderful Sharon never gave up on my healing. She had joy. The kind that begins at your core and seems to radiate outward. I often told her I wanted that joy. For months before my sweetheart died, she and I had talked of her joy. She always said it was the joy of the Lord. Those were pretty words and I wanted to believe them. But with my love gone, I saw no hope of ever finding joy again—with or without God.

Sharon was not so easily daunted. She told me I could experience that joy in the middle of my crisis. I didn't share her optimism and hope. I thought I'd simply wither and cease to exist. I teetered atop an emotional precipice between staggering pain and complete numbness. I was quite sure there was no room in that place for joy.

Imagine you are playing in the ocean, rolling gently in the beautiful waves. The water is wonderfully refreshing. The ocean spray sparkles in the dazzling sunshine. You are thankful for your life and the joy of the moment. You feel happy and blessed. You feel the anchoring safety of the shoreline. But then you look up and see nothing but water on all sides. Suddenly the waves begin to feel menacing and you recognize something is terribly wrong.

You panic and paddle frantically, but with no sense of direction. Your endurance is faltering. You cry out for help, but there seems to be no one to hear you. You realize you could be overtaken by the next crashing wave and easily sink into the dark unknown deep. You are as alone as you have ever been in your life. You are aching with fatigue. Your heart and lungs are crushed with the effort to survive.

You are near giving up with the hopelessness of it all. Then, in a suspended moment, a calm comes over you. You hear a voice from way down in your spirit. It says, "when you go through deep water, I will be with you." Your body seems to rise up from the cold deep, pushing up and out into the bright sunshine. You ride the crest of a gentle wave right up onto the sandy beach. As you lie there, grateful to be saved, you recognize what you heard was your own spirit recalling Isaiah 43:2!

That is how I felt when I became aware that I could have joy again. I would begin by reading God's Word. Perhaps I'd known it all along, but I didn't really understand until one crystallized moment when I heard God's promise in my pain.

Now, you are going through your own personal pain. I really do understand. It is awful. Your situation may differ from our stories, but the emotional challenges are much the same. We are hurting women with a universal pain. It is sad, but there are so many of us out there who have been on the bumpy road you now travel. And sadder still is the fact that there are many more to come, with no apparent relief. The world needs healing for sure. But for right now, the focus is on you.

You can't know it now, but you will survive this and—here is a shocker—you will be joyful again! For now you are angry, disillusioned, frightened, confused, and maybe lost. Sadly, no one can go through this for you. The road ahead can be challenging, but here is something I hope you learn, if you learn nothing else: God will get you through with less bruising and scarring than if you attempt to go it without him.

Sharon and I feel a sisterhood with you. We hurt for you. We hope you will let us walk by your side as you seek God's healing . . . wisdom, love, and joy.

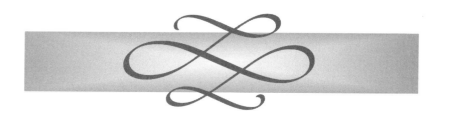

YOUR HEALING BEGINS

AM I LOVED?

If your husband told you he doesn't love you anymore, it stands to reason you may feel unloved and even unlovable. It is no small thing to be cast aside by the man you hoped to share the rest of your life with. The good news is, your Heavenly Father loves you more than you can possibly imagine in your wildest of wild dreams. It is breaking his heart that you are hurting and feeling unloved. Throughout the Bible, God's most profound message is his love for you.

I came to know God's love and thought it should be enough. Why then was there still such a yearning in my heart? God made me with human desires to love and be loved by another human. The most powerful covenant a human being can have is the covenant of marriage. It is the way God intended things to be. When God heals your heart, you may long to love, again. Let God choose your mate. He wants a Boaz for you. A Boaz man is a man who wants to be kind to you, to give you all he has. God wants a spiritually mature man who will cherish you for the wonder that is you.

". . . You are precious to me. You are honored, and I love you."
—Isaiah 43:4

PRAYER

Lord, I have never realized how much you truly love me. I feel so undeserving. The way my marriage ended left me feeling unworthy of anyone's love. I am sorry, Lord, that I let my husband convince me of my lack of worth. I feel hopeful for the first time in a very long time. I know if you love me, I have a brighter future ahead of me. Thank you, Lord, for loving me.

"All glory to him who loves us and has freed us from our sins by shedding his blood for us."

—Revelation 1:5

"'Don't be afraid,' he said, 'for you are very precious to God. Peace! Be encouraged! Be strong!'"

—Daniel 10:19

"'For the mountains may move and the hills disappear, but even then my faithful love for you will remain. My covenant of blessing will never be broken,' says the LORD*, who has mercy on you."*

—Isaiah 54:10

"How precious are your thoughts about me, O God. They cannot be numbered! I can't even count them; they outnumber the grains of sand! And when I wake up, you are still with me!"

—Psalm 139:17-18

"He turned the intended curse into a blessing because the LORD *your God loves you."*

—Deuteronomy 23:5

"'I have always loved you,' says the LORD*."*

—Malachi 1:2

"Now let your unfailing love comfort me, just as you promised me, your servant."

—Psalm 119:76

"Long ago the LORD *said to Israel: 'I have loved you, my people, with an everlasting love. With unfailing love I have drawn you to myself.'"*

—Jeremiah 31:3

"For the Lord *your God is living among you. He is a mighty savior. He will take delight in you with gladness. With his love, he will calm all your fears. He will rejoice over you with joyful songs."*

—Zephaniah 3:17

"This is real love—not that we loved God, but that he loved us and sent his Son as a sacrifice to take away our sins."

—1 John 4:10

"See, I have written your name on the palms of my hands."

—Isaiah 49:16

"No, despite all these things, overwhelming victory is ours through Christ, who loved us."

—Romans 8:37

"There I will go to the altar of God, to God—the source of all my joy. I will praise you with my harp, O God, my God!"

—Psalm 43:4

"You didn't choose me. I chose you. I appointed you to go and produce lasting fruit, so that the Father will give you whatever you ask for, using my name."

—John 15:16

"He escorts me to the banquet hall; it's obvious how much he loves me."

—Song of Songs 2:4

"I will be your God throughout your lifetime—until your hair is white with age. I made you, and I will care for you. I will carry you along and save you."

—Isaiah 46:4

"But God is so rich in mercy, and he loved us so much."

—Ephesians 2:4

"I love all who love me. Those who search will surely find me."

—Proverbs 8:17

"And I will give you treasures hidden in the darkness—secret riches. I will do this so you may know that I am the Lord, *the God of Israel, the one who calls you by name."*

—Isaiah 45:3

"And this hope will not lead to disappointment. For we know how dearly God loves us, because he has given us the Holy Spirit to fill our hearts with his love."

—Romans 5:5

"When God our Savior revealed his kindness and love, he saved us, not because of the righteous things we had done, but because of his mercy. He washed away our sins, giving us a new birth and new life through the Holy Spirit. He generously poured out the Spirit upon us through Jesus Christ our Savior. Because of his grace he declared us righteous and gave us confidence that we will inherit eternal life."

—Titus 3:4-7

"Now may our Lord Jesus Christ himself and God our Father, who loved us and by his grace gave us eternal comfort and a wonderful hope, comfort you and strengthen you in every good thing you do and say."

—2 Thessalonians 2:16-17

"For God loved the world so much that he gave his one and only Son, so that everyone who believes in him will not perish but have eternal life."

—John 3:16

- I feel alone; scared of being by myself scared of being without someone special in my life.
- Betrayed; angry; hurt; not able to understand how he could do this to me.
- I never stopped trying to help him but I did stop being in love with him. I fell out of love long ago. I knew this was not meant to be but I could not leave someone who was sick. Not until I found out he was with someone else. Whether friends or more trust was not there anymore and can never be found again. I realized I never truly knew the man I married. He was a stranger to me. That scared me. I never knew why he did it may never know maybe I was not there for him enough or did not listen enough but I was a good wife and did not deserve that. I will never look at him the same again...

Marriage & love is not about weddings, rings, dresses, etc. It is about your true love. The person who understands u, listens to you, loves you, completes you. Not sure I or we ever had that; I know I did not. I hope to one day find that man and the only thing that matters will be our love for each other.

GOD WANTS YOU TO FEEL HIS LOVE FOR YOU. IT IS COMPLETE.

*LOVE YOURSELF,
EAT ON THE
GOOD CHINA.*

ANGER

You read my ranting as I told my story earlier. I wasn't just angry. I was in a red-hot rage. Even when I was getting biblical wisdom, I had difficulty receiving it. The rage boiled up in the core of my being. I was seething with smothering resentment that seemed to consume me. Anger is understandable but futile, in that it is counterproductive. The issue with anger is the danger of speaking or acting out that anger. When we control ourselves, God loves, forgives, and consoles us.

Frankly, it was many months before I could think about my ex with anything but anger. I came to feel differently when God grew my heart. I knew God wanted me to pray for him. I was reluctantly obedient. Over time my heart softened towards my ex. I still don't approve of much of what he did. But I can better understand the hurt of his earlier life and what shaped the kind of man he became. God taught me a powerful lesson about how to deal with anger-producing issues and those that hurt me.

> *"And don't sin by letting anger control you. Don't let the sun go down while you are still angry, for anger gives a foothold to the devil."*
>
> —Ephesians 4:26-27

PRAYER

God, I am so mad. I can't seem to shake it off. I know my husband and my situation make me angry, but I hear you, God, when you tell me that my anger is a choice. I find myself telling my story over and over. I am choosing to talk about my marriage and divorce and keep my anger fresh and alive. I want a new story Lord. I want a fresh start, not fresh anger. Help me choose not to feed my own anger with the retelling of my old story. Help me settle this anger once and for all.

"Get rid of all bitterness, rage, anger, harsh words, and slander, as well as all types of evil behavior."

—Ephesians 4:31

"An angry person starts fights; a hot-tempered person commits all kinds of sin."

—Proverbs 29:22

"A hot-tempered person starts fights; a cool-tempered person stops them."

—Proverbs 15:18

"Stop being angry! Turn from your rage! Do not lose your temper—it only leads to harm."

—Psalm 37:8

"People with understanding control their anger; a hot temper shows great foolishness."

—Proverbs 14:29

"Yet for my own sake and for the honor of my name, I will hold back my anger and not wipe you out."

—Isaiah 48:9

"But now is the time to get rid of anger, rage, malicious behavior, slander, and dirty language."

—Colossians 3:8

"Understand this, my dear brothers and sisters: You must all be quick to listen, slow to speak, and slow to get angry. Human anger does not produce the righteousness God desires."

—James 1:19-20

"Control your temper, for anger labels you a fool."

—Ecclesiastes 7:9

"A gentle answer deflects anger, but harsh words make tempers flare."

—Proverbs 15:1

"Sensible people control their temper; they earn respect by overlooking wrongs."

—Proverbs 19:11

"But you, O LORD, *are a shield around me; you are my glory, the one who holds my head high."*

—Psalm 3:3

"The LORD *is compassionate and merciful, slow to get angry and filled with unfailing love."*

—Psalm 103:8

"Short-tempered people do foolish things, and schemers are hated."

—Proverbs 14:17

"Better to be patient than powerful; better to have self-control than to conquer a city."

—Proverbs 16:32

"Since God chose you to be the holy people he loves, you must clothe yourselves with tenderhearted mercy, kindness, humility, gentleness, and patience."

—Colossians 3:12

"Don't befriend angry people or associate with hot-tempered people, or you will learn to be like them and endanger your soul."

—Proverbs 22:24-25

"For the Scriptures say, 'If you want to enjoy life and see many happy days, keep your tongue from speaking evil and your lips from telling lies.'"

—1 Peter 3:10

I could not deal with the crazy anymore I could not even stand the sight of him around me it literally made me physically ill. I thought it best to cut him out of my life completely. That worked for many months now seeing him again I realize I have so many questions I want to ask him so many "Whys" but then I realize I will never get those answers; never the truth; and I get a sickening feeling in my stomach. Maybe better not to know just move on ... Chris never told the truth about anything I learned shortly after we were married. I think he had so many dark secrets and mental issues he lived in another reality he lied so much. These lies hurt and I was so tired of lying for him to my family & friends to make everything look normal - it wasn't far from it. At least now in my life the lying is over but knowing bc we have Dum we will have to be in each others lives forever is makes my heart sink. I love my son you cant regret having a child but it is an awful + confusing feeling to regret ever meeting his father.

I wonder why God put Chris in my life. I always asked To send me An angel and I for a long time thought he was the one... I dont now. I havent for a long time.

GOD KNOWS YOUR ANGER AND HE UNDERSTANDS.

PLANT FLOWERS IN YOUR YARD.

BROKEN-HEARTEDNESS

I knew the heart's function was to pump life-giving blood through my body. Then the common valentine sentiment suggests love originates in the heart. I subscribe to both beliefs. So when my heart began that shattering, explosive breaking, the fear it would no longer serve me was real. I would squeeze my own chest in an effort to hold all the broken pieces together. When I felt that crushing pressure, I didn't know it was my spirit being crushed.

If you haven't experienced a broken heart, you can only wonder how it might feel. If you have had that experience, the word "broken" carries new meaning for you. It is a physical pain like no other. I wish I could spare you that awful feeling. But it is done now. What is left is for God to mend your heart with his precious love. Each word of scripture can be another stitch that mends what man did to you; each word, a balm for your crushed spirit; each word a testament to what God has for you and that broken heart of yours.

"A broken heart crushes the spirit."

—Proverbs 15:13

PRAYER

My heart feels so broken and shattered. I feel fragmented, unhinged, in the deepest pain I've ever felt. It takes my breath away. Lord, I thank you for your healing words. I know I need only to read them to begin the healing of my broken heart. Word by word and piece by piece you will rebuild my heart and make it whole, once again.

"The Spirit of the Sovereign LORD is upon me, for the LORD has anointed me to bring good news to the poor. He has sent me to comfort the brokenhearted and to proclaim that captives will be released and prisoners will be freed."

—Isaiah 61:1

"My heart is confident in you, O God; my heart is confident. No wonder I can sing your praises! Wake up, my heart! Wake up, O lyre and harp! I will wake the dawn with my song."

—Psalm 57:7-8

"Search me, O God, and know my heart; test me and know my anxious thoughts."

—Psalm 139:23

"Laughter can conceal a heavy heart, but when the laughter ends, the grief remains."

—Proverbs 14:13

"A peaceful heart leads to a healthy body; jealousy is like cancer in the bones."

—Proverbs 14:30

"And I will give them one heart and one purpose: to worship me forever, for their own good and for the good of all their descendants."

—Jeremiah 32:39

"The LORD is my strength and shield. I trust him with all my heart. He helps me, and my heart is filled with joy. I burst out in songs of thanksgiving."

—Psalm 28:7

"Guard your heart above all else, for it determines the course of your life."

—Proverbs 4:23

"He heals the brokenhearted and bandages their wounds."

—Psalm 147:3

"The LORD *is close to the brokenhearted; he rescues those whose spirits are crushed."*

—Psalm 34:18

"Why am I discouraged? Why is my heart so sad? I will put my hope in God! I will praise him again—my Savior and my God!"

—Psalm 42:5-6

"God's word lives in your hearts, and you have won your battle with the evil one."

—1 John 2:14

"Purify me from my sins, and I will be clean; wash me, and I will be whiter than snow."

—Psalm 51:7

"I am leaving you with a gift—peace of mind and heart. And the peace I give is a gift the world cannot give. So don't be troubled or afraid."

—John 14:27

"Oh, give me back my joy again; you have broken me—now let me rejoice."

—Psalm 51:8

"As Saul turned and started to leave, God gave him a new heart, and all Samuel's signs were fulfilled that day."

—1 Samuel 10:9

"And the Father who knows all hearts knows what the Spirit is saying, for the Spirit pleads for us believers in harmony with God's own will."

—Romans 8:27

"And I will give you a new heart, and I will put a new spirit in you. I will take out your stony, stubborn heart and give you a tender, responsive heart."

—Ezekiel 36:26

"Those who have been ransomed by the LORD *will return. They will enter Jerusalem singing, crowned with everlasting joy. Sorrow and mourning will disappear, and they will be filled with joy and gladness."*

—Isaiah 51:11

"Don't let your hearts be troubled. Trust in God, and trust also in me."

—John 14:1

*"'*LORD, *help!' they cried in their trouble, and he saved them from their distress. He sent out his word and healed them, snatching them from the door of death. Let them praise the* LORD *for his great love and for the wonderful things he has done for them. Let them offer sacrifices of thanksgiving and sing joyfully about his glorious acts."*

—Psalm 107:19-22

"The young women will dance for joy, and the men—old and young—will join in the celebration. I will turn their mourning into joy. I will comfort them and exchange their sorrow for rejoicing."

—Jeremiah 31:13

I felt that pain of a broken heart it was deep and so bad I fell to my knees many times. It was overwhelming no idea what to do. You feel helpless like a knife just pierced it. That pain did subside but every now + then it comes back when I least expect it. I don't think I feel anything for Chris anymore > Anger is all that's left. My heart still hurts not for him but for my life and now I want and need to move on. How scared I am to have a future alone. To have to rebuild my heart scared that it may get hurt again > Michael. I have so many mixed feelings for him pain, joy, stability, I feel secure in his arms. But the pain I felt that Thurs. night cut me to the bone and put me back to Chris again. I need his companionship in my life right now but I am not sure about a relationship not sure my heart can take more pain. Accepting what Chris did to me is going to take time and running into a new relationship cannot mask the pain. As I realized it is only temporary and when something

does happen it leaves me with even more
pain & hurt, Refer to the quote
"Guard your heart above all else because
it determines the course of your life"
God help me to guard it And know
when to let that guard down.

GOD HEALS WHAT MAN HAS BROKEN.

SEND A CARD TO A HURTING FRIEND.

COMFORT

I define comfort in many ways. On a winter's night it might be a roaring fire and a fuzzy afghan. On a warm sunny day it is the feeling of my toes in the sand and the sun on my face. But it is always the sense of wellness, an ease of certainty. And a knowing that all is well and you didn't make it so. It is the calm of knowing and accepting life's moments. It is a gift God bestows on you because you love him and he loves you.

When you seek God's comfort, he goes to work. He doesn't fix all your problems and whip up a perfect life for you. Rather, God talks to your spirit, the place inside you that feels frazzled and out of control. God speaks words of rest and ease, love and assurance, peace and love. He offers you comfort in exchange for your willingness to rest in him. There is comfort in knowing God has you, that nothing is too great for him, that all things are possible, because he strengthens you. What you need is comfort and God is there to hold you.

> *"Now let your unfailing love comfort me, just as you promised me, your servant."*
>
> —Psalm 119:76

PRAYER

Will I ever feel safe and comfortable again? I feel so vulnerable. My life seems to have breaks and skips in it. It is no longer a continuous thread winding and turning through my days and weeks and months. My life is a broken line with skips and angles going in multiple directions. I don't feel secure, Lord. Calm my discomfort and show me that I can rest in you.

Remind me that you are certain—not chaotic; you are peace—not strife; you are harmony—not mayhem. I want to rest, Lord, and let you do the work.

"So be truly glad. There is wonderful joy ahead, even though you have to endure many trials for a little while."

—1 Peter 1:6

"Give all your worries and cares to God, for he cares about you."

—1 Peter 5:7

"Your promise revives me; it comforts me in all my troubles."

—Psalm 119:50

"I will be your God throughout your lifetime—until your hair is white with age. I made you, and I will care for you. I will carry you along and save you."

—Isaiah 46:4

"Sing for joy, O heavens! Rejoice, O earth! Burst into song, O mountains! For the LORD *has comforted his people and will have compassion on them in their suffering."*

—Isaiah 49:13

"All praise to God, the Father of our Lord Jesus Christ. God is our merciful Father and the source of all comfort. He comforts us in all our troubles so that we can comfort others. When they are troubled, we will be able to give them the same comfort God has given us."

—2 Corinthians 1:3-4

"I will comfort you there in Jerusalem as a mother comforts her child."

—Isaiah 66:13

"Even when I walk through the darkest valley, I will not be afraid, for you are close beside me. Your rod and your staff protect and comfort me."

—Psalm 23:4

"If you look for me wholeheartedly, you will find me."

—Jeremiah 29:13

"'As surely as my new heavens and earth will remain, so will you always be my people, with a name that will never disappear,' says the LORD."

—Isaiah 66:22

"As soon as I pray, you answer me; you encourage me by giving me strength."

—Psalm 138:3

"'For I know the plans I have for you,' says the LORD. 'They are plans for good and not for disaster, to give you a future and a hope.'"

—Jeremiah 29:11

"God blesses those who mourn, for they will be comforted."

—Matthew 5:4

"When three of Job's friends heard of the tragedy he had suffered, they got together and traveled from their homes to comfort and console him. Their names were Eliphaz the Temanite, Bildad the Shuhite, and Zophar the Naamathite."

—Job 2:11

"Now may our Lord Jesus Christ himself and God our Father, who loved us and by his grace gave us eternal comfort and a wonderful hope, comfort you and strengthen you in every good thing you do and say."

—2 Thessalonians 2:16-17

"The young women will dance for joy, and the men—old and young—will join in the celebration. I will turn their mourning into joy. I will comfort them and exchange their sorrow for rejoicing."

—Jeremiah 31:13

"I, yes I, am the one who comforts you. So why are you afraid of mere humans, who wither like the grass and disappear?"

—Isaiah 51:12

"I will comfort those who mourn, bringing words of praise to their lips."

—Isaiah 57:18-19

"When doubts filled my mind, your comfort gave me renewed hope and cheer."

—Psalm 94:19

"He lifted me out of the pit of despair, out of the mud and the mire. He set my feet on solid ground and steadied me as I walked along."

—Psalm 40:2

"From the ends of the earth, I cry to you for help when my heart is overwhelmed. Lead me to the towering rock of safety, for you are my safe refuge, a fortress where my enemies cannot reach me. Let me live forever in your sanctuary, safe beneath the shelter of your wings!"

—Psalm 61:2-4

Lord I do not feel safe & comfortable anymore and I long to be in someones arms that gives me those feelings. I thought I found those feelings with Michael > not sure. I can honestly say I did not have those feelings with Chris I always felt like I had to take care of everything and be the one to make everything calm + safe. I hopes that I can experience these feelings when someone wraps their arms around me.

GOD FEELS YOUR PAIN AND IT SADDENS HIM.

TREAT YOURSELF TO A PEDICURE.

CONTROLLING YOUR MOUTH

I have been brought to my knees by cruel and unjust words spoken against me. So it should have been very apparent to me, what harm I could do with my mouth. I know I have some things to repent for. I say to you—this is not the time for gossip. This includes the gossip you listen to. It may be helpful news from well-meaning friends or family. But listening to what others say can bring consequences of it's own.

Guard your mouth. If it is negative . . . don't say it. This also includes negative things you say over yourself. I remember a friend nearly slapped me when I said, "no one will ever love me again." She had already learned what it means to control the mouth. The tongue is a powerful instrument for good or harm. Good and kind words build the listener up, bridge gaps in understanding, heal hurts, and express value. Gossip, mean-spirited talk, and insults only erode the soul of the listener and the speaker.

"The tongue can bring death or life."

—Proverbs 18:21

PRAYER

I have so many hateful things in my heart that my mouth wants to say. It is especially difficult when I encounter someone who wants to engage in talk about what I am going through. Lord, help me to smile in those times. Help me to say, "with God's help, I am getting through." Help me to answer inquiries with, "thank you for asking, but I am no longer looking back, only ahead."

"I said to myself, 'I will watch what I do and not sin in what I say. I will hold my tongue when the ungodly are around me.'"

—Psalm 39:1

"Wise words satisfy like a good meal; the right words bring satisfaction. The tongue can bring death or life; those who love to talk will reap the consequences."

—Proverbs 18:20-21

"And when you are brought to trial in the synagogues and before rulers and authorities, don't worry about how to defend yourself or what to say, for the Holy Spirit will teach you at that time what needs to be said."

—Luke 12:11-12

"Again I say, don't get involved in foolish, ignorant arguments that only start fights."

—2 Timothy 2:23

"I will praise the LORD *at all times. I will constantly speak his praises."*

—Psalm 34:1

"For my words are wise, and my thoughts are filled with insight."

—Psalm 49:3

"For I will give you the right words and such wisdom that none of your opponents will be able to reply or refute you!"

—Luke 21:15

"Those who control their tongue will have a long life; opening your mouth can ruin everything."

—Proverbs 13:3

"The king is pleased with words from righteous lips; he loves those who speak honestly."

—Proverbs 16:13

"Everyone enjoys a fitting reply; it is wonderful to say the right thing at the right time!"

—Proverbs 15:23

"Indeed, we all make many mistakes. For if we could control our tongues, we would be perfect and could also control ourselves in every other way."

—James 3:2

"Kind words are like honey—sweet to the soul and healthy for the body."

—Proverbs 16:24

"You must not pass along false rumors. You must not cooperate with evil people by lying on the witness stand."

—Exodus 23:1

"A truly wise person uses few words; a person with understanding is even-tempered."

—Proverbs 17:27

"Now go! I will be with you as you speak, and I will instruct you in what to say."

—Exodus 4:12

"Let your conversation be gracious and attractive so that you will have the right response for everyone."

—Colossians 4:6

"Watch your tongue and keep your mouth shut, and you will stay out of trouble."

—Proverbs 21:23

"The words of the godly are a life-giving fountain; the words of the wicked conceal violent intentions."

—Proverbs 10:11

"Then keep your tongue from speaking evil and your lips from telling lies!"

—Psalm 34:13

"Take control of what I say, O Lord, and guard my lips. Don't let me drift toward evil or take part in acts of wickedness. Don't let me share in the delicacies of those who do wrong."

—Psalm 141:3-4

"Some people make cutting remarks, but the words of the wise bring healing. Truthful words stand the test of time, but lies are soon exposed. The Lord detests lying lips, but he delights in those who tell the truth."

—Proverbs 12:18-19,22

"The words you say will either acquit you or condemn you."

—Matthew 12:37

"For the Scriptures say, 'If you want to enjoy life and see many happy days, keep your tongue from speaking evil and your lips from telling lies.'"

—1 Peter 3:10

I need to try And remain calm, speak without emotion, be fair on friday. I have not spoken or seen him in months > when I did see him I felt nothing. Not hatred not love ...nothing. Its like a dark void when I look at him. Then I wonder how I could have ever loved him... A stranger a person I never knew. That is the only painful feeling I have left. For my sons sake so we can all move on I will try my best to be quiet and not say any evil things.

God I ask for your help to become detached from the situation and able to control my tongue and feelings. Amen.

SILENCE IS TRULY GOLDEN.

TELL SOMEONE YOU APPRECIATE THEM.

CRYING

I thought I would never stop crying. Everything set me off. Silent tears burning their relentless track down my face, was my most frequent cry. A fleeting thought, a song, a memory, or nothing at all could produce tears I often couldn't explain. Sometimes, my crying became fevered, loud, wailing, ugly, and messy. All the emotions like anger and resentment and jealousy translated to deep, powerful hurt that couldn't be satisfied without tears.

I didn't want to cry, but there was no stopping the physical need to release the pain and tension. And never would I suggest you not cry about something so tragic happening in your life. I've heard it said that crying is helpful and even a necessary release. It is the washing away of the soiled, unholy, sad result of the end of love. Even Jesus wept. So by all means, let it out. I just wish I could put my arm around you, when your tears come. One thing I know for sure. . . .

"He hears the cry of the needy."

—Job 34:28

PRAYER

Lord, I am not ready to stop crying. I have so much pain that needs to come out. I can't even keep my tears private. They come suddenly, unexpectedly, and with little provocation. Soon, Lord, soon. I pray my tears begin to dry up; that the washing away of the soil of divorce is swift and thorough. I ask that joy would return to my face. Lord, I pray that I will no longer look the part of the victim. I know you hear my cries and my prayers.

"I weep with sorrow; encourage me by your word."

—Psalm 119:28

"They cause the poor to cry out, catching God's attention. He hears the cries of the needy."

—Job 34:28

"But you, O Lord, are a shield around me; you are my glory, the one who holds my head high."

—Psalm 3:3

"Listen to my cry for help, my King and my God, for I pray to no one but you."

—Psalm 5:2

"Go away, all you who do evil, for the Lord has heard my weeping."

—Psalm 6:8

"For he who avenges murder cares for the helpless. He does not ignore the cries of those who suffer."

—Psalm 9:12

"Lord, you know the hopes of the helpless. Surely you will hear their cries and comfort them."

—Psalm 10:17

"O Lord, hear my plea for justice. Listen to my cry for help. Pay attention to my prayer, for it comes from honest lips."

—Psalm 17:1

"But in my distress I cried out to the Lord; yes, I prayed to my God for help. He heard me from his sanctuary; my cry to him reached his ears."

—Psalm 18:6

"For he has not ignored or belittled the suffering of the needy. He has not turned his back on them, but has listened to their cries for help."

—Psalm 22:24

"Listen to my prayer for mercy as I cry out to you for help, as I lift my hands toward your holy sanctuary."

—Psalm 28:2

"For his anger lasts only a moment, but his favor lasts a lifetime! Weeping may last through the night, but joy comes with the morning."

—Psalm 30:5

"I waited patiently for the Lord to help me, and he turned to me and heard my cry."

—Psalm 40:1

"Morning, noon, and night I cry out in my distress, and the Lord hears my voice."

—Psalm 55:17

"O Lord, God of my salvation, I cry out to you by day. I come to you at night. Now hear my prayer; listen to my cry."

—Psalm 88:1-2

"Those who plant in tears will harvest with shouts of joy. They weep as they go to plant their seed, but they sing as they return with the harvest."

—Psalm 126:5-6

"From the depths of despair, O Lord, I call for your help. Hear my cry, O Lord. Pay attention to my prayer."

—Psalm 130:1-2

"O Lord, I am calling to you. Please hurry! Listen when I cry to you for help!"

—Psalm 141:1

"He grants the desires of those who fear him; he hears their cries for help and rescues them."

—Psalm 145:19

"He will swallow up death forever! The Sovereign Lord will wipe away all tears. He will remove forever all insults and mockery against his land and people. The Lord has spoken!"

—Isaiah 25:8

"My tears flow endlessly; they will not stop until the Lord looks down from heaven and sees."

—Lamentations 3:49-50

"I have seen what they do, but I will heal them anyway! I will lead them. I will comfort those who mourn, bringing words of praise to their lips."

—Isaiah 57:18-19

"He will wipe every tear from their eyes, and there will be no more death or sorrow or crying or pain. All these things are gone forever."

—Revelation 21:4

Pain > Crying
I've blocked out so much of when it happened in January but this past month has been hard for me. When Michael canceled plans I felt myself in that dark place again my heart shattered ... again. I cried, yelled, screamed, broke things. I will never understand why it brought back so many bad feelings but it did. I hate crying it makes me hurt that means to remember and right now thats too painful. A song comes to mind "Let her go" from Passenger. The day I heard this song I cried my eyes out the pain in my heart was too much but everytime its on I still listen and cry relentlessly > it is a release and i need to cry more to let the pain out so I can move on and heal myself ... maybe one day forgive him.

GO AHEAD AND CRY—
IT'S CLEANSING.
GOD WILL DRY
YOUR TEARS WITH
HIS LOVE.

HOLD A SWEET BABY.

DO GOOD WH[illegible] YOU HEAL

No way! I had nothing to give anyone. I was depleted of all good, all energy, all love, and all caring. I never actually said it. But I thought it. Fortunately, no one asked me to show a kindness to someone, because that would have been my response. Are you feeling the same? Believe me, I get it. When I was in the depths of my despair, I thought I couldn't—or shouldn't—give a piece of my fragmented self to anyone. But honestly, seeking opportunities to do good and following through is good, godly, and therapeutic.

I was months into my divorce battle when my friend said, "go buy a gallon of milk and give it to someone at the grocery store." I thought she was crazy. "Who do I give it to?" I asked. All she said was, "you'll know." So I did as she suggested. The receiver of the milk said, "You can't imagine how much I need this." Such a simple act! I came away from that experience feeling obedient to God's prompting and able to meet someone else's need.

"Oh, the joys of those who are kind to the poor! The Lord rescues them when they are in trouble."

—Psalm 41:1

PRAYER

I believe it, Lord, when I read that I will feel better if I can give of myself. So many friends and family rushed to my aid when my husband filed. They cried with me, held me up when I hadn't the strength. They brought food, sent notes and emails, made phone calls, and dropped in to check on me. Each effort, no matter how small, helped me cope and now help me heal. I want to be that kind of a blessing to someone else. Lord, show me how to take the focus off myself and how I can be loving and helpful to another.

> *"So let's not get tired of doing what is good. At just the right time we will reap a harvest of blessing if we don't give up. Therefore, whenever we have the opportunity, we should do good to everyone—especially to those in the family of faith."*
>
> —Galatians 6:9-10

> *"Don't be concerned for your own good but for the good of others."*
>
> —1 Corinthians 10:24

> *"Don't be selfish; don't try to impress others. Be humble, thinking of others as better than yourselves. Don't look out only for your own interests, but take an interest in others, too."*
>
> —Philippians 2:3-4

> *"And don't forget to do good and to share with those in need. These are the sacrifices that please God."*
>
> —Hebrews 13:16

> *"Whoever gives to the poor will lack nothing, but those who close their eyes to poverty will be cursed."*
>
> —Proverbs 28:27

> *"Blessed are those who are generous, because they feed the poor."*
>
> —Proverbs 22:9

"Feed the hungry, and help those in trouble. Then your light will shine out from the darkness, and the darkness around you will be as bright as noon."

—Isaiah 58:10

"Work with enthusiasm, as though you were working for the Lord rather than for people. Remember that the Lord will reward each one of us for the good we do, whether we are slaves or free."

—Ephesians 6:7-8

"Those who shut their ears to the cries of the poor will be ignored in their own time of need."

—Proverbs 21:13

"Remember this good deed, O my God, and do not forget all that I have faithfully done for the Temple of my God and its services."

—Nehemiah 13:14

"But to you who are willing to listen, I say, love your enemies! Do good to those who hate you."

—Luke 6:27

"If you help the poor, you are lending to the LORD*—and he will repay you!"*

—Proverbs 19:17

"When God's people are in need, be ready to help them. Always be eager to practice hospitality."

—Romans 12:13

"And God will generously provide all you need. Then you will always have everything you need and plenty left over to share with others. As the Scriptures say, 'They share freely and give generously to the poor. Their good deeds will be remembered forever.'"

—2 Corinthians 9:8-9

"Blessed are those who help the poor."

—Proverbs 14:21

"Don't let evil conquer you, but conquer evil by doing good."

—Romans 12:21

"Good comes to those who lend money generously and conduct their business fairly."

—Psalm 112:5

"But as for you, be strong and courageous, for your work will be rewarded."

—2 Chronicles 15:7

YOUR HEART WILL HEAL EVEN FASTER IF YOU DO SOMETHING FOR SOMEONE ELSE WHO IS HURTING.

TIP YOUR WAITRESS WELL.

ENEMIES

If your husband was unfaithful, filed for divorce, or has ownership in misdeeds associated with your marriage and divorce, he is probably enemy number one. How sad for you if family and friends also take sides, making you enemies, as well.

It is so easy to step into hateful thinking about each other. Divorce splits more than husbands and wives. Children, family, and friends may be divided or asked to rally around one spouse over the other. They often try to show support by bringing up past hurts or violations your husband did against you. I encourage you not to listen. It is understandable from their point of view, but it serves no purpose for you to listen.

You have your enemy, if that is how you see your husband and those who support him. God commands us to pray for our enemies. God knows destructive behavior can lead to nothing but destruction. Follow God's command to pray for the wrongdoers and see the right he will make of it.

"For the Lord your God is the one who goes with you to fight for you against your enemies to give you victory."

—Deuteronomy 20:4 NIV

PRAYER

I wish I could pray that someone would run over my ex-husband. It's not a very Christian prayer, but when it comes to my enemies, I don't feel very Christian. He is my biggest enemy just now and I feel like making him pay for what he did to me. Lord, you have had so much worse done to you. Help me put this in perspective. Help me to take my hands off of any retaliation. Help me to leave the matter in your hands.

"Oh, please help us against our enemies, for all human help is useless. With God's help we will do mighty things, for he will trample down our foes."

—Psalm 108:12-13

"The eternal God is your refuge, and his everlasting arms are under you. He drives out the enemy before you."

—Deuteronomy 33:27

"He rescued me from my powerful enemies, from those who hated me and were too strong for me."

—2 Samuel 22:18

"My eyes are always on the Lord, for he rescues me from the traps of my enemies."

—Psalm 25:15

"But I say, love your enemies! Pray for those who persecute you! In that way, you will be acting as true children of your Father in heaven. For he gives his sunlight to both the evil and the good, and he sends rain on the just and the unjust alike."

—Matthew 5:44-45

"God blesses you when people mock you and persecute you and lie about you and say all sorts of evil things against you because you are my followers."

—Matthew 5:11

"Don't be afraid of the enemy! Remember the Lord, who is great and glorious, and fight for your brothers, your sons, your daughters, your wives, and your homes!"

—Nehemiah 4:14

"Then I will hold my head high above my enemies who surround me. At his sanctuary I will offer sacrifices with shouts of joy, singing and praising the Lord *with music."*

—Psalm 27:6

"You must worship only the Lord *your God. He is the one who will rescue you from all your enemies."*

—2 Kings 17:39

"The Lord *protects the foreigners among us. He cares for the orphans and widows, but he frustrates the plans of the wicked."*

—Psalm 146:9

"I have heard the many rumors about me, and I am surrounded by terror. My enemies conspire against me, plotting to take my life. But I am trusting you, O Lord, saying, 'You are my God!' My future is in your hands. Rescue me from those who hunt me down relentlessly."

—Psalm 31:13-15

"Though I am surrounded by troubles, you will protect me from the anger of my enemies. You reach out your hand, and the power of your right hand saves me."

—Psalm 138:7

"You are the one who gives us victory over our enemies; you disgrace those who hate us."

—Psalm 44:7

"My enemies will retreat when I call to you for help. This I know: God is on my side!"

—Psalm 56:9

"Hear my cry, for I am very low. Rescue me from my persecutors, for they are too strong for me."

—Psalm 142:6

"In your unfailing love, silence all my enemies and destroy all my foes, for I am your servant."

—Psalm 143:12

"We have been rescued from our enemies so we can serve God without fear."

—Luke 1:74

"I will rescue you from those you fear so much."

—Jeremiah 39:17

"I called on the LORD*, who is worthy of praise, and he saved me from my enemies."*

—Psalm 18:3

"I trust in you, my God! Do not let me be disgraced, or let my enemies rejoice in my defeat."

—Psalm 25:2

"May the evil plans of my enemies be turned against them. Do as you promised and put an end to them."

—Psalm 54:5

"O God, listen to my complaint. Protect my life from my enemies' threats."

—Psalm 64:1

"You have seen the wrong they have done to me, LORD*. Be my judge, and prove me right. You have seen the vengeful plots my enemies have laid against me."*

—Lamentations 3:59-60

PRAY FOR YOUR ENEMIES . . . IT WILL IRRITATE SATAN.

SMILE AT A STRANGER.

FAVOR

I truly didn't understand favor for a very long time. But with time and Bible study comes wisdom. Favor is my new fave! Did you ever imagine you could ask God for favor? It's true, you can. You can ask all who love you to pray, and pray yourself, for God to give you favor in legal matters, in your finances, for a job search, virtually anything.

God loves, loves, loves to provide for us. There is absolutely no restriction on what God can do for you, opening doors of opportunity, bringing a new man into your life, allowing for your tiniest or most magnificent longing to be realized. If your desires align with God's plan for you, His favor will straighten paths, light your way, smooth out hurdles, open doors, and cause mighty things to happen.

So when you ask, be bold. Know that with God, all things are possible. He will supernaturally open doors for you. Watch him work in your life. How cool is God?

"For whoever finds me finds life and receives favor from the Lord."
—Proverbs 8:35 NIV

PRAYER

I love this one, Lord. How wonderful that you show me favor, ever, about anything! I can pray about favor on any matter and you hear my prayer. Now is a good time for me to call on some of that favor. I have so many concerns and needs as a result of my divorce. I need favor in so many areas. Lord, I put before you the concerns of just today. Please grant me favor in the matters I will confront on this day.

"What's more, I am with you, and I will protect you wherever you go. One day I will bring you back to this land. I will not leave you until I have finished giving you everything I have promised you."

—Genesis 28:15

"Stay on the path that the Lord your God has commanded you to follow. Then you will live long and prosperous lives in the land you are about to enter and occupy."

—Deuteronomy 5:33

"Seek the Kingdom of God above all else, and live righteously, and he will give you everything you need."

—Matthew 6:33

"And now that you belong to Christ, you are the true children of Abraham. You are his heirs, and God's promise to Abraham belongs to you."

—Galatians 3:29

"All praise to God, the Father of our Lord Jesus Christ, who has blessed us with every spiritual blessing in the heavenly realms because we are united with Christ."

—Ephesians 1:3

"Your favor, O LORD, *made me as secure as a mountain. Then you turned away from me, and I was shattered."*

—Psalm 30:7

"If you search for good, you will find favor; but if you search for evil, it will find you!"

—Proverbs 11:27

"May the LORD *show you his favor and give you his peace."*

—Numbers 6:26

"Then you will find favor with both God and people, and you will earn a good reputation."

—Proverbs 3:4

"Instead of shame and dishonor, you will enjoy a double share of honor. You will possess a double portion of prosperity in your land, and everlasting joy will be yours."

—Isaiah 61:7

"The LORD *says, 'I will give you back what you lost to the swarming locusts, the hopping locusts, the stripping locusts, and the cutting locusts.'"*

—Joel 2:25

"If you listen to these commands of the LORD *your God that I am giving you today, and if you carefully obey them, the* LORD *will make you the head and not the tail, and you will always be on top and never at the bottom."*

—Deuteronomy 28:13

"And may the Lord our God show us his approval and make our efforts successful. Yes, make our efforts successful!"

—Psalm 90:17

"When Job prayed for his friends, the LORD *restored his fortunes. In fact, the* LORD *gave him twice as much as before!"*

—Job 42:10

"He has sent me to tell those who mourn that the time of the LORD*'s favor has come, and with it, the day of God's anger against their enemies."*

—Isaiah 61:2

"Uzziah sought God during the days of Zechariah, who taught him to fear God. And as long as the king sought guidance from the LORD*, God gave him success."*

—2 Chronicles 26:5

"O LORD my God, you have performed many wonders for us. Your plans for us are too numerous to list. You have no equal. If I tried to recite all your wonderful deeds, I would never come to the end of them."

—Psalm 40:5

"I will open the windows of heaven for you. I will pour out a blessing so great you won't have enough room to take it in!"

—Malachi 3:10

"May God be merciful and bless us. May his face smile with favor on us."

—Psalm 67:1

"For nothing is impossible with God."

—Luke 1:37

"The thief's purpose is to steal and kill and destroy. My purpose is to give them a rich and satisfying life."

—John 10:10

"'Don't be afraid, Mary,' the angel told her, 'for you have found favor with God!'"

—Luke 1:30

"So the LORD blessed Job in the second half of his life even more than in the beginning."

—Job 42:12

"Day by day the LORD takes care of the innocent, and they will receive an inheritance that lasts forever. They will not be disgraced in hard times; even in famine they will have more than enough."

—Psalm 37:18-19

"Peace and prosperity to you, your family, and everything you own!"

—1 Samuel 25:6

ASK GOD FOR FAVOR AND BLESSINGS IN YOUR EVERYDAY LIFE.

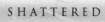

BAKE A PIE FOR A NEIGHBOR.

FEAR

Fear, oh yes—another of my constant companions. I feared absolutely everything. This was uncharted territory, after all. Even my first divorce didn't give me confidence to get me through the second. The unknown is cause for trepidation. My future was as unknown to me as yours is to you.

There are so many uncertainties when your household is in upheaval. Someone is moving out, possessions are being fought over, friends are shocked, and families are upset. Everything is in turmoil. Your ability to unclutter your mind and see what needs to be done is impossible. It is all so scary.

No matter what I say, you are still going to be fearful. So don't listen to me, listen to your Creator. He says you have no need to fear at all. Following his will is safe footing. Know that if you keep your focus on him, unwaveringly, he will show you that your fear is unfounded. He is your soft place to fall. Let him quell your fears.

"Don't be afraid, I am here."

—John 6:20

PRAYER

You know how scared I am, God. I am fearful about everything. My once-certain life has proved to be uncertain. I never dreamed I would have to face so many fears all at once. I am gripped with the inability to make the smallest decision because of my fear. Not knowing what is ahead used to seem like the spice and adventure in life. Now it is just scary. I hesitate to take even the smallest step for fear it is not forward, but backward. I know you don't want me to suffer with this kind of fear. I know I am equipped to handle anything you ask of me. I know I am able to take care of myself. I may have to make some adjustments, but I know I can do this. Lord, I pray you will calm my fears, allowing me to do what I have to do for myself.

"Listen to me, you who know right from wrong, you who cherish my law in your hearts. Do not be afraid of people's scorn, nor fear their insults."

—Isaiah 51:7

"But I will rescue you from those you fear so much."

—Jeremiah 39:17

"This is my command—be strong and courageous! Do not be afraid or discouraged. For the LORD *your God is with you wherever you go."*

—Joshua 1:9

"Don't be afraid of anyone's anger, for the decision you make is God's decision. Bring me any cases that are too difficult for you, and I will handle them."

—Deuteronomy 1:17

"Don't be afraid of the enemy! Remember the Lord, who is great and glorious, and fight for your brothers, your sons, your daughters, your wives, and your homes!"

—Nehemiah 4:14

"But Jesus spoke to them at once. 'Don't be afraid,' he said. 'Take courage. I am here!'"

—Matthew 14:27

"But Jesus overheard them and said to Jairus, 'Don't be afraid. Just have faith.'"

—Mark 5:36

"'Don't be afraid,' he said, 'for you are very precious to God. Peace! Be encouraged! Be strong!'"

—Daniel 10:19

"Be strong and courageous, and do the work. Don't be afraid or discouraged, for the LORD *God, my God, is with you. He will not fail you or forsake you."*

—1 Chronicles 28:20

"But Moses told the people, 'Don't be afraid. Just stand still and watch the LORD *rescue you today. The Egyptians you see today will never be seen again.'"*

—Exodus 14:13

"So be strong and courageous! Do not be afraid and do not panic before them. For the LORD *your God will personally go ahead of you. He will neither fail you nor abandon you."*

—Deuteronomy 31:6

"This is what the LORD *says: Do not be afraid! Don't be discouraged by this mighty army, for the battle is not yours, but God's."*

—2 Chronicles 20:15

"For God has not given us a spirit of fear and timidity, but of power, love, and self-discipline."

—2 Timothy 1:7

"On that day the announcement to Jerusalem will be, 'Cheer up, Zion! Don't be afraid! For the LORD *your God is living among you. He is a mighty savior. He will take delight in you with gladness. With his love, he will calm all your fears. He will rejoice over you with joyful songs.'"*

—Zephaniah 3:16-17

"I know the LORD *is always with me. I will not be shaken, for he is right beside me."*

—Psalm 16:8

"No, do not be afraid of those nations, for the LORD *your God is among you, and he is a great and awesome God."*

—Deuteronomy 7:21

"But when Jesus heard what had happened, he said to Jairus, 'Don't be afraid. Just have faith, and she will be healed.'"

—Luke 8:50

"Fearing people is a dangerous trap, but trusting the LORD *means safety."*

—Proverbs 29:25

"Even when I walk through the darkest valley, I will not be afraid, for you are close beside me. Your rod and your staff protect and comfort me."

—Psalm 23:4

"But even if you suffer for doing what is right, God will reward you for it. So don't worry or be afraid of their threats."

—1 Peter 3:14

"You will be safe from slander and have no fear when destruction comes."

—Job 5:21

"'Do not fear the king of Babylon anymore,' says the LORD. *'For I am with you and will save you and rescue you from his power.'"*

—Jeremiah 42:11

"Son of man, do not fear them or their words. Don't be afraid even though their threats surround you like nettles and briers and stinging scorpions. Do not be dismayed by their dark scowls, even though they are rebels."

—Ezekiel 2:6

"They were all terrified when they saw him. But Jesus spoke to them at once. 'Don't be afraid,' he said. 'Take courage! I am here!'"

—Mark 6:50

DO NOT BE AFRAID, GOD IS YOUR PROTECTOR.

SING ALONG WITH THE RADIO.

FORGIVENESS

Forgiveness feels nearly impossible. The damage is so acute. The desire to forgive just isn't there. That's why Jesus died for our sins. He wanted there to be no doubt—we were forgiven. I believe the most godly thing we can do is to forgive those who hurt us. Without a forgiving heart, we keep our broken-heartedness fresh and hurting. Forgiving will release the pain.

Please know forgiveness doesn't mean approval. Of course God doesn't want us to approve of behavior that is not biblical and leads to divorce. But God does want us to heal and he knows forgiveness will bring healing.

A wise pastor once said that harboring unforgiveness is like taking poison and hoping our enemies die. Unforgiveness will thwart our spiritual growth and prevent peace and joy from fully returning to our lives. Forgiving doesn't mean approving of what was done to you. It is simply releasing the responsibility of thinking about it one more minute. It is giving the matter to God. It is refusing to relive the emotion that resulted from the violation. It is vowing to move beyond the past, clearing the junk from your path, not looking back, not wallowing in what won't propel you forward.

"He canceled the record of charges against us and took it away by nailing it to the cross."

—Colossians 2:14

PRAYER

I don't want to forgive him or her or them. I never, never, never want to. But scripture commands me to. The forgiveness is not for them. That should make it easier, God. You tell me the forgiveness is for my benefit. I know if I make up my mind to forgive them, you will cause my emotions to catch up with my forgiveness commitment. Lord, I want to be able to look back and feel no hostility toward my ex-husband or his lady friend. That is a tall order from where I am standing now. But I know you will help me with this, Lord.

"I will never again remember their sins and lawless deeds."
—Hebrews 10:17

"I am writing to you who are God's children because your sins have been forgiven through Jesus."
—1 John 2:12

"He is so rich in kindness and grace that he purchased our freedom with the blood of his Son and forgave our sins."
—Ephesians 1:7

"He has removed our sins as far from us as the east is from the west."
—Psalm 103:12

"You were dead because of your sins and because your sinful nature was not yet cut away. Then God made you alive with Christ, for he forgave all our sins. He canceled the record of the charges against us and took it away by nailing it to the cross."
—Colossians 2:13-14

"My dear children, I am writing this to you so that you will not sin. But if anyone does sin, we have an advocate who pleads our case before the Father. He is Jesus Christ, the one who is truly righteous. He himself is the sacrifice that atones for our sins—and not only our sins but the sins of all the world."
—1 John 2:1-2

"I will cleanse them of their sins against me and forgive all their sins of rebellion."
—Jeremiah 33:8

"'Come now, let's settle this,' says the LORD. *'Though your sins are like scarlet, I will make them as white as snow. Though they are red like crimson, I will make them as white as wool.'"*

—Isaiah 1:18

"Do not judge others, and you will not be judged. Do not condemn others, or it will all come back against you. Forgive others, and you will be forgiven."

—Luke 6:37

"Make allowance for each other's faults, and forgive anyone who offends you. Remember, the Lord forgave you, so you must forgive others."

—Colossians 3:13

"Forgive us our sins, as we forgive those who sin against us."

—Luke 11:4

"But when you are praying, first forgive anyone you are holding a grudge against, so that your Father in heaven will forgive your sins, too."

—Mark 11:25

"But if we confess our sins to him, he is faithful and just to forgive us our sins and to cleanse us from all wickedness."

—1 John 1:9

"If you forgive those who sin against you, your heavenly Father will forgive you."

—Matthew 6:14

"Instead, be kind to each other, tenderhearted, forgiving one another, just as God through Christ has forgiven you."

—Ephesians 4:32

"Then Peter came to him and asked, 'Lord, how often should I forgive someone who sins against me? Seven times?' 'No, not seven times,' Jesus replied, 'but seventy times seven!'"

—Matthew 18:21-22

"Bless those who persecute you. Don't curse them; pray that God will bless them."

—Romans 12:14

"Once again you will have compassion on us. You will trample our sins under your feet and throw them into the depths of the ocean!"

—Micah 7:19

"Then if my people who are called by my name will humble themselves and pray and seek my face and turn from their wicked ways, I will hear from heaven and will forgive their sins and restore their land."

—2 Chronicles 7:14

"He forgives all my sins and heals all my diseases."

—Psalm 103:3

"I—yes, I alone—will blot out your sins for my own sake and will never think of them again."

—Isaiah 43:25

"Let the wicked change their ways and banish the very thought of doing wrong. Let them turn to the LORD *that he may have mercy on them. Yes, turn to our God, for he will forgive generously."*

—Isaiah 55:7

"The LORD *is slow to anger and filled with unfailing love, forgiving every kind of sin and rebellion."*

—Numbers 14:18

"Purify me from my sins, and I will be clean; wash me, and I will be whiter than snow."

—Psalm 51:7

FORGIVE, FORGIVE, FORGIVE. IT IS A DECISION AND WELL WORTH THE EFFORT.

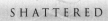

TAKE THE NEIGHBOR'S NEWSPAPER UP TO THEIR DOOR.

THE FUTURE

My good woman, hear God tell you over and over: he has plans for you. Your future is bright, shiny, and new. Your future is about growth, excellence, and wonder. God promises you prosperity, love, peace, joy, and forgiveness. You are his precious daughter, whom he loves so deeply. He wants all the best for you.

He wants you to feel the healing, know his love, and have a song in your heart. He wants you to dance with the joy of being alive and doing his will. God wants you to shout to the world that you are adored by your Heavenly Father and he is the best father in the world. God wants your future to be dazzling, fulfilling, and blessed. He promises to hear you and address all your needs. He wants you to know that you simply have to claim those promises. God, the God of the universe, made those promises to *you*. There is no better plan or guarantee for what is ahead for you.

> *"For I know the plans I have for you, says the Lord. They are plans for good and not for disaster, to give you a future and a hope."*
>
> —Jeremiah 29:11

PRAYER

I can't even think about the future. Today is all the challenge I can handle. But your beautiful scriptures say you have a bright future for me. Promise, joy, peace, prosperity, forgiveness, growth, excellence, and wonder. How amazing to imagine any of those things in my life. I am not experiencing those blessings yet, but I know I will. I suppose it would not be called my "future" if it were my "now." Thank you, Lord, for the anticipation I am enjoying right now.

"For he raised us from the dead along with Christ and seated us with him in the heavenly realms because we are united with Christ Jesus. So God can point to us in all future ages as examples of the incredible wealth of his grace and kindness toward us, as shown in all he has done for us who are united with Christ Jesus."

—Ephesians 2:6-7

"'For I know the plans I have for you,' says the LORD. *'They are plans for good and not for disaster, to give you a future and a hope. In those days when you pray, I will listen. If you look for me wholeheartedly, you will find me.'"*

—Jeremiah 29:11-13

"The LORD *will work out his plans for my life—for your faithful love,* O LORD, *endures forever. Don't abandon me, for you made me."*

—Psalm 138:8

"I don't mean to say that I have already achieved these things or that I have already reached perfection. But I press on to possess that perfection for which Christ Jesus first possessed me. No, dear brothers and sisters, I have not achieved it, but I focus on this one thing: Forgetting the past and looking forward to what lies ahead."

—Philippians 3:12:13

"But forget all that—it is nothing compared to what I am going to do. For I am about to do something new. See, I have already begun! Do you not see it? I will make a pathway through the wilderness. I will create rivers in the dry wasteland."

—Isaiah 43:18-19

"Such things were written in the Scriptures long ago to teach us. And the Scriptures give us hope and encouragement as we wait patiently for God's promises to be fulfilled."

—Romans 15:4

"So be truly glad. There is wonderful joy ahead, even though you have to endure many trials for a little while."

—1 Peter 1:6

"My future is in your hands."

—Psalm 31:15

"Look at those who are honest and good, for a wonderful future awaits those who love peace."

—Psalm 37:37

"'There is hope for your future,' says the LORD. *'Your children will come again to their own land.'"*

—Jeremiah 31:17

"Look straight ahead, and fix your eyes on what lies before you."

—Proverbs 4:25

"You have allowed me to suffer much hardship, but you will restore me to life again and lift me up from the depths of the earth."

—Psalm 71:20

"Yet what we suffer now is nothing compared to the glory he will reveal to us later. For all creation is waiting eagerly for that future day when God will reveal who his children really are. . . . With eager hope, the creation looks forward to the day when it will join God's children in glorious freedom from death and decay."

—Romans 8:18-19,21

"This vision is for a future time. It describes the end, and it will be fulfilled. If it seems slow in coming, wait patiently, for it will surely take place. It will not be delayed."

—Habakkuk 2:3

"That is what the Scriptures mean when they say, 'No eye has seen, no ear has heard, and no mind has imagined what God has prepared for those who love him.' But it was to us that God revealed these things by his Spirit. For his Spirit searches out everything and shows us God's deep secrets."

—1 Corinthians 2:9-10

"But those who trust in the LORD *will find new strength. They will soar high on wings like eagles. They will run and not grow weary. They will walk and not faint."*

—Isaiah 40:31

"And I am certain that God, who began the good work within you, will continue his work until it is finally finished on the day when Christ Jesus returns."

—Philippians 1:6

"Now you have every spiritual gift you need as you eagerly wait for the return of our Lord Jesus Christ. He will keep you strong to the end so that you will be free from all blame on the day when our Lord Jesus Christ returns. God will do this, for he is faithful to do what he says, and he has invited you into partnership with his Son, Jesus Christ our Lord."

—1 Corinthians 1:7-9

"The LORD *keeps watch over you as you come and go, both now and forever."*

—Psalm 121:8

"'Yes,' Jesus replied, 'and I assure you that everyone who has given up house or brothers or sisters or mother or father or children or property, for my sake and for the Good News, will receive now in return a hundred times as many houses, brothers, sisters, mothers, children, and property—along with persecution. And in the world to come that person will have eternal life. But many who are the greatest now will be least important then, and those who seem least important now will be the greatest then.'"

—Mark 10:29-31

FORGET YESTERDAY—
IT DOESN'T BELONG
IN YOUR FUTURE.
THE VERY BEST IS
AHEAD OF YOU.

TIDY UP YOUR JUNK DRAWER.

GOD IS WITH YOU

God is at your side, loving you and hurting for you. God wants you to talk to him, in the here and now. He is there for those times when you feel set apart, no longer a Mrs., but a Ms. in a room full of people and yet still so alone.

I was often at a family function surrounded by people who loved me, but I felt so disconnected. I would forget that God never leaves us for a single moment. We are never alone. He is such a gentleman, that you'd hardly notice him there. But he is always at the ready to come to our aid, to comfort us, to assure us, to help us decide, to fight temptation . . . whatever we need. We need only to speak to him. He is always waiting to hear from us. He wants to know everything we think, feel, see, and hear. He never tires of hearing from us. I would have been comforted if I had known.

"Be sure of this, I am with you always."

Matthew 28:20

PRAYER

Lord, I am reading so many wonderful things I never fully understood or appreciated. But learning you are here is the most wonderful of all. I always thought of you as everywhere or nearby or just a prayer away. But you are here, right *here* with me. You never leave me. I thought you left to take care of more important people or matters and came when I called with a major crisis or confession. I was so wrong. You are with me always, Lord. Every moment of every hour of every day, you are *in* me waiting to have a chat. I am never alone!

"The Lord will not abandon his people, because that would dishonor his great name. For it has pleased the Lord to make you his very own people."

—1 Samuel 12:22

"And when I wake up, you are still with me!"

—Psalm 139:18

"I know the LORD *is always with me. I will not be shaken, for he is right beside me."*

—Psalm 16:8

"The LORD *himself watches over you! The* LORD *stands beside you as your protective shade."*

—Psalm 121:5

"O Israel, can I not do to you as this potter has done to his clay? As the clay is in the potter's hand, so are you in my hand."

—Jeremiah 18:6

"For God has said, 'I will never fail you. I will never abandon you.'"

—Hebrews 13:5

"When you go through deep waters, I will be with you. When you go through rivers of difficulty, you will not drown. When you walk through the fire of oppression, you will not be burned up; the flames will not consume you."

—Isaiah 43:2

"Listen, all you people of Judah and Benjamin! The LORD *will stay with you as long as you stay with him! Whenever you seek him, you will find him. But if you abandon him, he will abandon you."*

—2 Chronicles 15:2

"This is my command—be strong and courageous! Do not be afraid or discouraged. For the Lord your God is with you wherever you go."

—Joshua 1:9

"So be strong and courageous! Do not be afraid and do not panic before them. For the LORD *your God will personally go ahead of you. He will neither fail you nor abandon you."*

—Deuteronomy 31:6

"But from there you will search again for the LORD *your God. And if you search for him with all your heart and soul, you will find him."*

—Deuteronomy 4:29

"Even if my father and mother abandon me, the LORD *will hold me close."*

—Psalm 27:10

"Come close to God, and God will come close to you. Wash your hands, you sinners; purify your hearts, for your loyalty is divided between God and the world."

—James 4:8

"Then when you call, the Lord will answer. 'Yes, I am here,' he will quickly reply. Remove the heavy yoke of oppression. Stop pointing your finger and spreading vicious rumors! Feed the hungry, and help those in trouble. Then your light will shine out from the darkness, and the darkness around you will be as bright as noon. The Lord will guide you continually, giving you water when you are dry and restoring your strength. You will be like a well-watered garden, like an ever-flowing spring."

—Isaiah 58:9-11

"The LORD *keeps watch over you as you come and go, both now and forever."*

—Psalm 121:8

"Don't be afraid, for I am with you. Don't be discouraged, for I am your God. I will strengthen you and help you. I will hold you up with my victorious right hand."

—Isaiah 41:10

"For the Lord *your God is living among you. He is a mighty savior. He will take delight in you with gladness. With his love, he will calm all your fears. He will rejoice over you with joyful songs."*

—Zephaniah 3:17

"When you go out to fight your enemies and you face horses and chariots and an army greater than your own, do not be afraid. The Lord *your God, who brought you out of the land of Egypt, is with you!"*

—Deuteronomy 20:1

"For I hold you by your right hand—I, the Lord *your God. And I say to you, 'Don't be afraid. I am here to help you.'"*

—Isaiah 41:13

"God arms me with strength, and he makes my way perfect. He makes me as surefooted as a deer, enabling me to stand on mountain heights. He trains my hands for battle; he strengthens my arm to draw a bronze bow. You have given me your shield of victory. Your right hand supports me; your help has made me great."

—Psalm 18:32-35

LET THE LORD CARRY YOU. HE DOESN'T WANT YOU TO DO THIS ALONE—AND YOU DON'T HAVE TO!

WATCH THE WONDER OF A SUNRISE.

GUILT

What a useless emotion. The list of things that might bring about the sting of guilt is endless. I think this emotion is Satan's favorite. Let's face it, he wants us miserable, frustrated, scared, and feeling guilty. Guilt is the fortified soil Satan plants his seed in. Guilt erodes the spirit, disconnects you from God, turns your face away from those who love you and want to help you. Guilt is a negative emotion that serves no one. It puts a wedge between you and the God that forgives you of whatever you are guilty of.

Satan must have been thrilled with me. I not only harbored guilt for what I did wrong, but also for the right I didn't do. As long as I remained in guilt, I couldn't see the sun, I couldn't feel joy, and I couldn't find hope. I thought I deserved to stay condemned. I beat myself up over and over and over. God wants to lift back the heavy, damp, oppressive blanket of guilt from us. It is his gift to the sinner.

> *"Oh, what joy those whose disobedience is forgiven, whose sin is put out of sight!"*
>
> —Psalm 32:1

Not my words, but God's. How awesome is our God? Just sayin.'

PRAYER

I have so much I have done wrong—everywhere and in everything. I have been beating myself up over it all. Lord, I am confessing my guilt. Wash me of my sin, Lord. I can ask forgiveness from whomever my sin might have hurt, but only you can remove my guilt, Lord.

"I will cleanse them of their sins against me and forgive all their sins of rebellion."

—Jeremiah 33:8

"Oh, what joy for those whose disobedience is forgiven, whose sin is put out of sight! Yes, what joy for those whose record the LORD *has cleared of guilt, whose lives are lived in complete honesty!"*

—Psalm 32:1-2

"Even if we feel guilty, God is greater than our feelings, and he knows everything."

—1 John 3:20

"Instead of shame and dishonor, you will enjoy a double share of honor. You will possess a double portion of prosperity in your land, and everlasting joy will be yours."

—Isaiah 61:7

"Wash me clean from my guilt. Purify me from my sin. . . . Purify me from my sins, and I will be clean; wash me, and I will be whiter than snow."

—Psalm 51:2,7

"Finally, I confessed all my sins to you and stopped trying to hide my guilt. I said to myself, 'I will confess my rebellion to the Lord.' And you forgave me! All my guilt is gone."

—Psalm 32:5

"For if you return to the Lord, your relatives and your children will be treated mercifully by their captors, and they will be able to return to this land. For the Lord your God is gracious and merciful. If you return to him, he will not continue to turn his face from you."

—2 Chronicles 30:9

GUILT

"He touched my lips with it and said, 'See, this coal has touched your lips. Now your guilt is removed, and your sins are forgiven.'"

—Isaiah 6:7

"Oh, what joy for those whose disobedience is forgiven, whose sins are put out of sight. Yes, what joy for those whose record the Lord has cleared of sin."

—Romans 4:7-8

"Where is another God like you, who pardons the guilt of the remnant, overlooking the sins of his special people? You will not stay angry with your people forever, because you delight in showing unfailing love."

—Micah 7:18

"You forgave the guilt of your people—yes, you covered all their sins."

—Psalm 85:2

"So now there is no condemnation for those who belong to Christ Jesus. And because you belong to him, the power of the life-giving Spirit has freed you from the power of sin that leads to death."

Romans 8:1-2

"'And they will not need to teach their neighbors, nor will they need to teach their relatives, saying, "You should know the Lord." For everyone, from the least to the greatest, will know me already,' says the Lord. 'And I will forgive their wickedness, and I will never again remember their sins.'"

—Jeremiah 31:34

"For the person who keeps all of the laws except one is as guilty as a person who has broken all of God's laws."

—James 2:10

"But the Lord will redeem those who serve him. No one who takes refuge in him will be condemned."

—Psalm 34:22

"Though we are overwhelmed by our sins, you forgive them all."

—Psalm 65:3

GUILT IS USELESS.
RELEASE IT NOW.

PUT A LITTLE EXTRA IN THE OFFERING PLATE.

JOY

Seriously, am I really suggesting you feel joy in any of this? Well, yes I am. When you are feeling every negative emotion served up with uncertainty, complications, and frustrations, joy is the last thing you are inclined to feel. It is a tough one to be sure. I was advised to let the joy return. What? Let the joy return? That sounded unreasonable and Pollyanna. And what's this about *let?* I didn't believe joy was an option I could choose. I'd always thought joy was what you felt when all was well and happy.

My always-happy friend danced into my kitchen saying, "This is the day the Lord has made and I will rejoice in it." She even hung the saying over my kitchen sink. All I thought, when I read it each day, was, *If God made this day, why is it so lousy?* Then one day I was reminded of this saying, "I complained I had no shoes, until I saw the man who had no feet." Joy wasn't about having all I wanted, but all I needed. It was a choice that was fully my own. It hit me full-force that finding joy simply brings more joy. It is not about being happy in your circumstances, but joyful in the Lord. I pray you get this lesson much faster than I did. God wants us to know joy even when we don't feel joy.

"Don't be dejected and sad, for the joy of the Lord is your strength."
—Nehemiah 8:10

PRAYER

Lord, I am stronger than I thought. I am already feeling more joy than when my junk started. Rejection is a joy-crusher, but through this process I have learned so much. I am stronger than I thought. I can do more, handle more, and find joy more easily.

Thank you, Lord, for bringing me through my drama and out into the light of joy.

"So rejoice in the LORD and be glad, all you who obey him! Shout for joy, all you whose hearts are pure!"

—Psalm 32:11

"I will shout for joy and sing your praises, for you have ransomed me."

—Psalm 71:23

"Instead of shame and dishonor, you will enjoy a double share of honor. You will possess a double portion of prosperity in your land, and everlasting joy will be yours."

—Isaiah 61:7

"Those who have been ransomed by the LORD will return. They will enter Jerusalem singing, crowned with everlasting joy. Sorrow and mourning will disappear, and they will be filled with joy and gladness."

—Isaiah 35:10

"Always be full of joy in the Lord. I say it again—rejoice!"

—Philippians 4:4

"So you have sorrow now, but I will see you again; then you will rejoice, and no one can rob you of that joy."

—John 16:22

"But the Holy Spirit produces this kind of fruit in our lives: love, joy, peace, patience, kindness, goodness, faithfulness."

—Galatians 5:22

"Come, everyone! Clap your hands! Shout to God with joyful praise!"
—Psalm 47:1

"Light shines on the godly, and joy on those whose hearts are right."
—Psalm 97:11

"This is the day the LORD *has made. We will rejoice and be glad in it."*
—Psalm 118:24

"A glad heart makes a happy face; a broken heart crushes the spirit."
—Proverbs 15:13

"A cheerful heart is good medicine, but a broken spirit saps a person's strength."
—Proverbs 17:22

"For the despondent, every day brings trouble; for the happy heart, life is a continual feast."
—Proverbs 15:15

"We were filled with laughter, and we sang for joy. And the other nations said, 'What amazing things the LORD *has done for them.'"*
—Psalm 126:2

"Shout with joy to the LORD, *all the earth! Worship the* LORD *with gladness. Come before him, singing with joy."*
—Psalm 100:1-2

"I am overwhelmed with joy in the LORD *my God! For he has dressed me with the clothing of salvation and draped me in a robe of righteousness. I am like a bridegroom in his wedding suit or a bride with her jewels."*
—Isaiah 61:10

"I have told you these things so that you will be filled with my joy. Yes, your joy will overflow!"

—John 15:11

"And Sarah declared, 'God has brought me laughter. All who hear about this will laugh with me.'"

—Genesis 21:6

"Always be joyful. Never stop praying."

—1 Thessalonians 5:16-17

"The humble will be filled with fresh joy from the Lord*. The poor will rejoice in the Holy One of Israel."*

—Isaiah 29:19

"Yet I will rejoice in the Lord*! I will be joyful in the God of my salvation!"*

—Habakkuk 3:18

"But let all who take refuge in you rejoice; let them sing joyful praises forever. Spread your protection over them, that all who love your name may be filled with joy."

—Psalm 5:11

FIND JOY IN THE LORD,
FOR HE FINDS
JOY IN YOU.

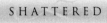

RENT A FUNNY MOVIE.

JEALOUSY

I could snatch her bald! Oh yes, I was guilty of that unholy thought. I hated to think of her in my bed. Cooking with my pans and bathing in my tub. My jealousy sat in the pit of my stomach like some sour, vile thing. My nastiest thoughts came from my jealousy. I knew, for the first time in my life, what it was to truly want what someone else had. It was once mine but now it was hers.

Jealousy isn't made right because of the unjust way you lost and someone else gained. Jealousy is the rust of the heart, a longing for what you had to let go of. Because you feel justified longing to have what once belonged to you, it will be nearly impossible to rid yourself of this one without God's help. The best of intentions (of which I had none), will fail unless you ask God to take the jealousy from you. Repeat this scripture often.

> *"Then at last my fury against you will be spent and my jealous anger will subside. I will be calm and will not be angry with you anymore."*
>
> —Ezekiel 16:42

PRAYER

I feel consumed by intense jealousy. I don't know why I even care, but I do. I am sick with it and sick of it. It feels corrosive, like it is eating away at my flesh, my heart, my resolve, my confidence, and my faith. I know I would feel happy and whole again, if only this jealousy were gone. Lord, help me heal and purge this jealousy from me.

"When you follow the desires of your sinful nature, the results are very clear: sexual immorality, impurity, lustful pleasures, idolatry, sorcery, hostility, quarreling, jealousy, outbursts of anger, selfish ambition, dissension, division, envy, drunkenness, wild parties, and other sins like these. . . . Let us not become conceited, or provoke one another, or be jealous of one another."

—Galatians 5:19-21,26

"Be still in the presence of the LORD, *and wait patiently for him to act. Don't worry about evil people who prosper or fret about their wicked schemes."*

—Psalm 37:7

"So don't be dismayed when the wicked grow rich and their homes become ever more splendid."

—Psalm 49:16

"Then I realized that my heart was bitter, and I was all torn up inside. I was so foolish and ignorant—I must have seemed like a senseless animal to you. Yet I still belong to you; you hold my right hand. You guide me with your counsel, leading me to a glorious destiny."

—Psalm 73:21-24

"Pay careful attention to your own work, for then you will get the satisfaction of a job well done, and you won't need to compare yourself to anyone else. For we are each responsible for our own conduct."

—Galatians 6:4-5

"So get rid of all evil behavior. Be done with all deceit, hypocrisy, jealousy, and all unkind speech."

—1 Peter 2:1

"Surely resentment destroys the fool, and jealousy kills the simple. I have seen that fools may be successful for the moment, but then comes sudden disaster."

—Job 5:2-3

"But if you are bitterly jealous and there is selfish ambition in your heart, don't cover up the truth with boasting and lying. For jealousy and selfishness are not God's kind of wisdom. Such things are earthly, unspiritual, and demonic. For wherever there is jealousy and selfish ambition, there you will find disorder and evil of every kind."

—James 3:14-16

"Because we belong to the day, we must live decent lives for all to see. Don't participate in the darkness of wild parties and drunkenness, or in sexual promiscuity and immoral living, or in quarreling and jealousy."

—Romans 13:13

"Love is patient and kind. Love is not jealous or boastful or proud."

—1 Corinthians 13:4

"Then I observed that most people are motivated to success because they envy their neighbors. But this, too, is meaningless—like chasing the wind."

—Ecclesiastes 4:4

"Anger is cruel, and wrath is like a flood, but jealousy is even more dangerous."

—Proverbs 27:4

"Don't envy sinners, but always continue to fear the LORD.*"*

—Proverbs 23:17

"A peaceful heart leads to a healthy body; jealousy is like cancer in the bones."

—Proverbs 14:30

"Don't envy violent people or copy their ways."

—Proverbs 3:31

"Don't envy evil people or desire their company. For their hearts plot violence, and their words always stir up trouble."

—Proverbs 24:1-2

JEALOUSY KILLS
YOUR JOY.
IT IS SATAN'S WORK
AND IT DARKENS
YOUR SPIRIT.

BUILD YOURSELF A BOUQUET FOR YOUR TABLE.

JUSTICE

Oh dear, now we are getting down to it. Can you find anything just about the mess you are in? No, of course you can't. The whole ridiculous saga is unfair and the need to see justice done can be the reason you get up in the morning. Perhaps this will be the day someone pays for your troubles. The Bible says, an eye for an eye. You think, *I'd like to blacken an eye or two, right now.*

I bargained with God. If he would let me exact my kind of justice out on my ex and the other woman, I would never ask for another thing as long as I lived. I know you long to see justice, too. Precious, wounded woman, God will make all right again. I know what I know what I know. And I know our just God and his holy plan to mete out justice is perfect.

"The Lord says, I will give you back what you lost."

—Joel 2:25

PRAYER

I have to trust that you are a just God. I am learning to do that by reading all the wonderful promises, acts of love and kindness, forgiveness, and justice in the Bible. Justice is your business, Lord. I can go on with my life and not look back. You will take care of those who hurt me.

"The Lord himself will fight for you. Just stay calm."

—Exodus 14:14

"But the Lord *will not let the wicked succeed or let the godly be condemned when they are put on trial."*

—Psalm 37:33

"When you hear the blast of the trumpet, rush to wherever it is sounding. Then our God will fight for us!"

—Nehemiah 4:20

"I will be patient as the Lord *punishes me, for I have sinned against him. But after that, he will take up my case and give me justice for all I have suffered from my enemies. The* Lord *will bring me into the light, and I will see his righteousness."*

—Micah 7:9

"This is what the Lord says: 'Be just and fair to all. Do what is right and good, for I am coming soon to rescue you and to display my righteousness among you.'"

—Isaiah 56:1

"Each one of you will put to flight a thousand of the enemy, for the Lord *your God fights for you, just as he has promised."*

—Joshua 23:10

"Instead, I want to see a mighty flood of justice, an endless river of righteous living."

—Amos 5:24

"I have created the blacksmith who fans the coals beneath the forge and makes the weapons of destruction. And I have created the armies that destroy."

—Isaiah 54:16

"For the Lord loves justice, and he will never abandon the godly. He will keep them safe forever, but the children of the wicked will die."

—Psalm 37:28

"Look now; I myself am he! There is no other god but me! I am the one who kills and gives life; I am the one who wounds and heals; no one can be rescued from my powerful hand!"

—Deuteronomy 32:39

"So God replied, 'Because you have asked for wisdom in governing my people with justice and have not asked for a long life or wealth or the death of your enemies—I will give you what you asked for! I will give you a wise and understanding heart such as no one else has had or ever will have!'"

—1 Kings 3:11-12

"Learn to do good. Seek justice. Help the oppressed. Defend the cause of orphans. Fight for the rights of widows."

—Isaiah 1:17

"Lord, you are my lawyer! Plead my case! For you have redeemed my life. You have seen the wrong they have done to me, LORD. *Be my judge, and prove me right."*

—Lamentations 3:58-59

"I wish I were the judge. Then everyone could bring their cases to me for judgment, and I would give them justice!"

—2 Samuel 15:4

"But you are obsessed with whether the godless will be judged. Don't worry, judgment and justice will be upheld."

—Job 36:17

"The LORD *gives righteousness and justice to all who are treated unfairly."*

—Psalm 103:6

"For I, the LORD, love justice. I hate robbery and wrongdoing. I will faithfully reward my people for their suffering and make an everlasting covenant with them."

—Isaiah 61:8

"In his justice he will pay back those who persecute you."

—2 Thessalonians 1:6

"This is what the Lord says to Jerusalem: 'I will be your lawyer to plead your case, and I will avenge you. I will dry up her river, as well as her springs.'"

—Jeremiah 51:36

"You must not pass along false rumors. You must not cooperate with evil people by lying on the witness stand."

—Exodus 23:1

"Your throne, O God, endures forever and ever. You rule with a scepter of justice. You love justice and hate evil. Therefore God, your God, has anointed you, pouring out the oil of joy on you more than on anyone else."

—Psalm 45:6-7

"Let the whole world sing for joy, because you govern the nations with justice and guide the people of the whole world."

—Psalm 67:4

"He will give justice to the poor and make fair decisions for the exploited. The earth will shake at the force of his word, and one breath from his mouth will destroy the wicked."

—Isaiah 11:4

"Righteousness and justice are the foundation of your throne. Unfailing love and truth walk before you as attendants."

—Psalm 89:14

"Justice is a joy to the godly, but it terrifies evildoers."

—Proverbs 21:15

NO ONE GETS AWAY WITH ANYTHING— BECAUSE GOD SEES EVERYTHING.

TAKE A DRIVE IN THE COUNTRY.

THE PAST

The past is the doorway to all the negative emotions you are struggling to get through. When you relive details, it keeps the anger, jealousy, hurt, shame, and disappointment in the forefront. Dwelling in the past only serves us if we have no desire to move forward. But you have chosen to read this book for this reason. You want the business of your divorce to be relabeled from your current situation, to the past. You want it behind you. I pray you can metaphorically take what is done and box it up. The only reason to reopen that box is to put the things that are hurting you today, inside. Tomorrow those things will be your past. The quickest way to your future is to release that past.

> *"But I focus on this one thing: forgetting the past and looking forward to what lies ahead."*
>
> —Philippians 3:13

PRAYER

I dredge up my past constantly. I talk about it with my friends. It is so easy for me to dwell on my past misery. I don't like being stuck here. You offer hope, Lord, and hope is not in the past, but in the future. It is the promise of good things to come. It is the promise of you turning the bad into something positive. All my junk is in the past and all my hope is in the future. Help me, Lord, to keep my past behind me where it belongs.

"Instead, be very glad—for these trials make you partners with Christ in his suffering, so that you will have the wonderful joy of seeing his glory when it is revealed to all the world."

—1 Peter 4:13

"But Lot's wife looked back as she was following behind him, and she turned into a pillar of salt."

—Genesis 19:26

"Throw off your old sinful nature and your former way of life, which is corrupted by lust and deception."

—Ephesians 4:22

"God keeps such people so busy enjoying life that they take no time to brood over the past."

—Ecclesiastes 5:20

"This means that anyone who belongs to Christ has become a new person. The old life is gone; a new life has begun!"

—2 Corinthians 5:17

"But Jesus told him, 'Anyone who puts a hand to the plow and then looks back is not fit for the Kingdom of God.'"

—Luke 9:62

"Such things were written in the Scriptures long ago to teach us. And the Scriptures give us hope and encouragement as we wait patiently for God's promises to be fulfilled."

—Romans 15:4

"But forget all that—it is nothing compared to what I am going to do."

—Isaiah 43:18

"You will forget your misery; it will be like water flowing away."

—Job 11:16

"Look, the winter is past, and the rains are over and gone."

—Song of Songs 2:11

"Look! I am creating new heavens and a new earth, and no one will even think about the old ones anymore."

—Isaiah 65:17

"You should clothe yourselves instead with the beauty that comes from within, the unfading beauty of a gentle and quiet spirit, which is so precious to God."

—1 Peter 3:4

"What is more pleasing to the Lord: your burnt offerings and sacrifices or your obedience to his voice? Listen! Obedience is better than sacrifice, and submission is better than offering the fat of rams."

—1 Samuel 15:22

"When you were slaves to sin, you were free from the obligation to do right. And what was the result? You are now ashamed of the things you used to do, things that end in eternal doom. But now you are free from the power of sin and have become slaves of God. Now you do those things that lead to holiness and result in eternal life. For the wages of sin is death, but the free gift of God is eternal life through Christ Jesus our Lord."

—Romans 6:20-23

THE PAST IS EXACTLY THAT, THE PAST. LOOK AHEAD.

READ A BOOK IN THE SUNSHINE.

PEACE

Peace is the absence of struggling. Perhaps you remember the TV ad that had the plea, "Calgon, take me away." The commercial showed a frazzled, busy mom, retreating to her Calgon bath to soak away her stressful life. As she soaked, the yelling children, stack of bills, and the sink full of dishes seemed to lose their urgency. Her tense demeanor was replaced by a look of serenity. You could almost see her harsh day become soft, pliable, and doable. It was clear the woman would be fortified and ready to tackle whatever remaining challenges the day held.

If a bath product can do that, imagine what God offers for peace—by simply seeking his face! God's peace isn't fleeting and doesn't require a tub. You can surrender anywhere, anytime, whether en route to your court appearance, sorting through legal documents, working out your finances, or balancing all the details of your life. Stop, breathe, seek his face. Accept his peace. Leave your turmoil behind.

"I am leaving you with a gift—peace of mind and heart. And the peace I give is a gift the world cannot give."

—John 14:27

PRAYER

I read that there is peace that surpasses all understanding. I can't imagine that, but I want it. I don't think I will find that peace unless I take your Bible to heart. It isn't enough to read it, but I must get it down in my spirit. Lord, open me up and fill me with your love and scriptures.

"You will keep in perfect peace all who trust in you, all whose thoughts are fixed on you! . . . LORD, you will grant us peace; all we have accomplished is really from you."

—Isaiah 26:3,12

"For those who follow godly paths will rest in peace when they die."

—Isaiah 57:2

"You will be secure under a government that is just and fair. Your enemies will stay far away. You will live in peace, and terror will not come near."

—Isaiah 54:14

"Peace and prosperity to you!"

—Daniel 4:1

"Salt is good for seasoning. But if it loses its flavor, how do you make it salty again? You must have the qualities of salt among yourselves and live in peace with each other."

—Mark 9:50

"Glory to God in highest heaven, and peace on earth to those with whom God is pleased."

—Luke 2:14

"Work at living in peace with everyone, and work at living a holy life, for those who are not holy will not see the Lord."

—Hebrews 12:14

"I am writing to all of you in Rome who are loved by God and are called to be his own holy people. May God our Father and the Lord Jesus Christ give you grace and peace."

—Romans 1:7

"Therefore, since we have been made right in God's sight by faith, we have peace with God because of what Jesus Christ our Lord has done for us."

—Romans 5:1

"May God give you more and more grace and peace as you grow in your knowledge of God and Jesus our Lord."

—2 Peter 1:2

"Again I say, don't get involved in foolish, ignorant arguments that only start fights."

—2 Timothy 2:23

"And those who are peacemakers will plant seeds of peace and reap a harvest of righteousness."

—James 3:18

"Whenever you enter someone's home, first say, 'May God's peace be on this house.'"

—Luke 10:5

"Dear brothers and sisters, I close my letter with these last words: Be joyful. Grow to maturity. Encourage each other. Live in harmony and peace. Then the God of love and peace will be with you."

—2 Corinthians 13:11

"Turn away from evil and do good. Search for peace, and work to maintain it."

—1 Peter 3:11

"God blesses those who work for peace, for they will be called the children of God."

—Matthew 5:9

"The Lord *gives his people strength. The* Lord *blesses them with peace."*

—Psalm 29:11

"Those who love your instructions have great peace and do not stumble."

—Psalm 119:165

"Make every effort to keep yourselves united in the Spirit, binding yourselves together with peace."

—Ephesians 4:3

"And let the peace that comes from Christ rule in your hearts. For as members of one body you are called to live in peace. And always be thankful."

—Colossians 3:15

"Submit to God, and you will have peace; then things will go well for you."

—Job 22:21

"Now may the Lord of peace himself give you his peace at all times and in every situation. The Lord be with you all."

—2 Thessalonians 3:16

"And I will make a covenant of peace with them, an everlasting covenant. I will give them their land and increase their numbers, and I will put my Temple among them forever."

—Ezekiel 27:26

IT'S A HEAD THING.
PEACE IS CALMNESS
IN SPITE OF *YOUR*
CIRCUMSTANCES.

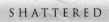

TAKE A FRIEND TO LUNCH.

PROTECTION

A lack of protection makes us vulnerable to powers that are greater than our own power to fight them. When we are made more fragile by the blows life hits us with, we are even less prepared to fight the battles that rage in the world. Praying for protection is a sure-fire way to insulate yourself from the devil, exes, hostile in-laws, the courtroom situation, temptation, physical harm, negative thinking, fear, and worry.

The Lord offers you his mighty protection for the asking. If he is for you, who can be against you? Why go through any part of your life—especially something like a divorce—without all of that protection God is offering?

"I trust in the Lord for protection."

—Psalm 11:1

PRAYER

Lord, I can't do this by myself. I have made so many mistakes—and look where it has landed me. I can't do this well, without your help. I need your protection, Lord. I need you to put a buffer around me to keep away all that can come against me. There is so much that is new to me, now. I don't want to do this without your help.

"Have mercy on me, O God, have mercy! I look to you for protection. I will hide beneath the shadow of your wings until the danger passes by. I cry out to God Most High, to God who will fulfill his purpose for me. He will send help from heaven to rescue me, disgracing those who hound me. My God will send forth his unfailing love and faithfulness."

—Psalm 57:1-3

"David sang this song to the Lord on the day the Lord rescued him from all his enemies and from Saul. He sang: 'The LORD is my rock, my fortress, and my savior; my God is my rock, in whom I find protection. He is my shield, the power that saves me, and my place of safety. He is my refuge, my savior, the one who saves me from violence. I called on the LORD, who is worthy of praise, and he saved me from my enemies.'"

—2 Samuel 22:1-4

"From the ends of the earth, I cry to you for help when my heart is overwhelmed. Lead me to the towering rock of safety, for you are my safe refuge, a fortress where my enemies cannot reach me. Let me live forever in your sanctuary, safe beneath the shelter of your wings!"

—Psalm 61:2-4

"The Lord protects all those who love him, but he destroys the wicked."

—Psalm 145:20

"What's more, I am with you, and I will protect you wherever you go. One day I will bring you back to this land. I will not leave you until I have finished giving you everything I have promised you."

—Genesis 28:15

"The LORD keeps you from all harm and watches over your life. The LORD keeps watch over you as you come and go, both now and forever."

—Psalm 121:7-8

"The LORD is my rock, my fortress, and my savior; my God is my rock, in whom I find protection. He is my shield, the power that saves me, and my place of safety."

—Psalm 18:2

"Keep me safe, O God, for I have come to you for refuge."

—Psalm 16:1

"Turn your ear to listen to me; rescue me quickly. Be my rock of protection, a fortress where I will be safe."

—Psalm 31:2

"The Lord *is my light and my salvation—so why should I be afraid? The* Lord *is my fortress, protecting me from danger, so why should I tremble?"*

—Psalm 27:1

"Though I am surrounded by troubles, you will protect me from the anger of my enemies. You reach out your hand, and the power of your right hand saves me."

—Psalm 138:7

"Protect me from wicked people who attack me, from murderous enemies who surround me."

—Psalm 17:9

"Though they stumble, they will never fall, for the Lord *holds them by the hand."*

—Psalm 37:24

"For you are my hiding place; you protect me from trouble. You surround me with songs of victory."

—Psalm 32:7

"'No, don't be afraid. I will continue to take care of you and your children.' So he reassured them by speaking kindly to them."

—Genesis 50:21

"God's way is perfect. All the Lord*'s promises prove true. He is a shield for all who look to him for protection."*

—2 Samuel 22:31

"The name of the LORD *is a strong fortress; the godly run to him and are safe."*

—Proverbs 18:10

"Fear of the LORD *leads to life, bringing security and protection from harm."*

—Proverbs 19:23

"He grants a treasure of common sense to the honest. He is a shield to those who walk with integrity. He guards the paths of the just and protects those who are faithful to him."

—Proverbs 2:7-8

"For I am with you, and no one will attack and harm you, for many people in this city belong to me."

—Acts 18:10

"Having hope will give you courage. You will be protected and will rest in safety."

—Job 11:18

"The eternal God is your refuge, and his everlasting arms are under you. He drives out the enemy before you; he cries out, 'Destroy them!'"

—Deuteronomy 33:27

"May the LORD *bless you and protect you."*

—Numbers 6:24

"He will cover you with his feathers. He will shelter you with his wings. His faithful promises are your armor and protection. . . . For he will order his angels to protect you wherever you go. . . . The LORD *says, 'I will rescue those who love me. I will protect those who trust in my name.'"*

—Psalm 91:4,11,14

BE BRAVE AND TAKE
THE NEXT STEP.
GOD WILL GUIDE YOU.

DRINK MORE WATER TODAY.

REJECTION

Rejection is a cold slap in the face. Even if the husband isn't someone you want anymore, his rejection stings, painfully. What's worse, is if he is a real creep and he rejects you, your self-esteem plummets. All I can say is, frankly, who cares if the creep doesn't want you? You are too special.

Precious Pastor Joel Osteen says it better then anyone, "you are the daughter of the most high God." Hmm, is it any wonder you aren't a suitable match for a creep? Why not choose to wear that rejection as a shield that says: he was not up to my standards, not worthy of my love, not in God's plan. He needed to move along making room for the man God has for you. And I hope you take comfort in the fact, God will never reject you. In fact . . .

> *"See how very much our Father loves us, for he calls us his children and that is what we are!"*
>
> —1 John 3:1

PRAYER

God, why do I care that I have been rejected? Why is rejection so painful? I know that pain too well. Help me to understand that my husband's rejection in no way defines me. You, Lord, accept me, and that is all that matters.

"And you belong to Christ, and Christ belongs to God."

—1 Corinthians 3:23

"Even if my father and mother abandon me, the L*ORD will hold me close."*

—Psalm 27:10

"Those who know your name trust in you, for you, O L*ORD, do not abandon those who search for you."*

—Psalm 9:10

"He was despised and rejected—a man of sorrows, acquainted with deepest grief. We turned our backs on him and looked the other way. He was despised, and we did not care. Yet it was our weaknesses he carried; it was our sorrows that weighed him down. And we thought his troubles were a punishment from God, a punishment for his own sins!"

—Isaiah 53:3-4

"Never again will you be called 'The Forsaken City' or 'The Desolate Land.' Your new name will be 'The City of God's Delight' and 'The Bride of God,' for the L*ORD delights in you and will claim you as his bride."*

—Isaiah 62:4

"When the poor and needy search for water and there is none, and their tongues are parched from thirst, then I, the L*ORD, will answer them. I, the God of Israel, will never abandon them."*

—Isaiah 41:17

"Yet Jerusalem says, 'The Lord has deserted us; the Lord has forgotten us.' 'Never! Can a mother forget her nursing child? Can she feel no love for the child she has borne? But even if that were possible, I would not forget you!'"

—Isaiah 49:14-15

"My sheep listen to my voice; I know them, and they follow me. I give them eternal life, and they will never perish. No one can snatch them away from me, for my Father has given them to me, and he is more powerful than anyone else. No one can snatch them from the Father's hand."

—John 10:27-29

"You didn't choose me. I chose you. I appointed you to go and produce lasting fruit, so that the Father will give you whatever you ask for, using my name."

—John 15:16

"What shall we say about such wonderful things as these? If God is for us, who can ever be against us?"

—Romans 8:31

"I will live among you, and I will not despise you. I will walk among you; I will be your God, and you will be my people."

—Leviticus 26:11-12

"For the Lord *your God is a merciful God; he will not abandon you or destroy you or forget the solemn covenant he made with your ancestors."*

—Deuteronomy 4:31

"So be strong and courageous! Do not be afraid and do not panic before them. For the Lord *your God will personally go ahead of you. He will neither fail you nor abandon you."*

—Deuteronomy 31:6

"And because we are his children, God has sent the Spirit of his Son into our hearts, prompting us to call out, 'Abba, Father.' Now you are no longer a slave but God's own child. And since you are his child, God has made you his heir."

—Galatians 4:6-7

"God decided in advance to adopt us into his own family by bringing us to himself through Jesus Christ. This is what he wanted to do, and it gave him great pleasure."

—Ephesians 1:5

GOD WILL NEVER REJECT YOU. THIS IS A PROMISE YOU CAN COUNT ON.

VOLUNTEER AT THE LOCAL ELEMENTARY SCHOOL.

SLEEPLESSNESS

So your mind is muddled chaos, your energy is depleted, you are seething with anger, you are fearful, in tears, and reviewing all your regrets. Is it any wonder you can't sleep? Been there and I am so sorry. Sweet slumber is exactly what you need just now. You know that of course, but what do you do to settle your mind, quell your fears, and get the rest your body needs?

It is all so simple to recognize what is keeping you awake. It is another matter entirely to find a solution while you are learning to manage the fear and uncertainty, jealousy and rage, regret and sorrow. Perhaps you wonder *what if it takes months to find enough peace to get any rest at all?* If you are so exhausted you can't even follow the scriptures for comfort, perhaps it is time to ask for a doctor's help. There are temporary measures available that can help you get some sleep. Then you can read and accept God's tender invitation for your peace and restoration.

"In peace I will lie down and sleep."

—Psalm 4:8

PRAYER

I lay in my bed in the darkness and struggle to turn off my life, like a light switch, and sleep. My tired, weary body aches from the emotional turmoil, the physical pain of sobbing for hours, the confusion about what is happening, the lack of focus to make the simplest future plans, and the empty desperation I feel. Remind me, Lord, that you are there. That I can release my concerns to you . . . and sleep.

"I will give you peace in the land, and you will be able to sleep with no cause for fear."

—Leviticus 26:6

"Those who live in the shelter of the Most High will find rest in the shadow of the Almighty. . . . Do not be afraid of the terrors of the night, nor the arrow that flies in the day."

—Psalm 91:1,5

"You can go to bed without fear; you will lie down and sleep soundly."

—Proverbs 3:24

"At this, I woke up and looked around. My sleep had been very sweet."

—Jeremiah 31:26

"For the LORD *has poured out on you a spirit of deep sleep."*

—Isaiah 29:10

"He lets me rest in green meadows; he leads me beside peaceful streams."

—Psalm 23:2

"The remnant of Israel will do no wrong; they will never tell lies or deceive one another. They will eat and sleep in safety, and no one will make them afraid."

—Zephaniah 3:13

"For God gives rest to his loved ones."

—Psalm 127:2

"The LORD *himself watches over you! The* LORD *stands beside you as your protective shade."*

—Psalm 121:5

"Then Jesus said, 'Come to me, all of you who are weary and carry heavy burdens, and I will give you rest.'"

—Matthew 11:28

"God's promise of entering his rest still stands, so we ought to tremble with fear that some of you might fail to experience it. . . . For only we who believe can enter his rest. As for the others, God said, 'In my anger I took an oath: "They will never enter my place of rest,"' even though this rest has been ready since he made the world. . . . For all who have entered into God's rest have rested from their labors, just as God did after creating the world. So let us do our best to enter that rest. But if we disobey God, as the people of Israel did, we will fall."

—Hebrews 4:1,3,10-11

"At sundown he arrived at a good place to set up camp and stopped there for the night. Jacob found a stone to rest his head against and lay down to sleep. As he slept, he dreamed of a stairway that reached from the earth up to heaven. And he saw the angels of God going up and down the stairway."

—Genesis 28:11-12

"People who work hard sleep well, whether they eat little or much. But the rich seldom get a good night's sleep."

—Ecclesiastes 5:12

"I lay down and slept, yet I woke up in safety, for the LORD *was watching over me."*

—Psalm 3:5

"Having hope will give you courage. You will be protected and will rest in safety. You will lie down unafraid, and many will look to you for help."

—Job 11:18-19

"One day soon afterward Jesus went up on a mountain to pray, and he prayed to God all night."

—Luke 6:12

"I think, 'My bed will comfort me, and sleep will ease my misery.'"

—Job 7:13

SATAN WILL KEEP YOU AWAKE. HE WANTS YOU VULNERABLE AND TIRED.

HAVE A LONG SOAK IN A WARM BATH.

A SOUND MIND

Is your brain on overdrive? Are you always thinking about what to do next? Where to go? Who to seek for help? What are the laws? What are the rules of the game?

I know my head would feel like a hollow space that had detail upon detail dumped in and all jumbled up. The zipping back and forth of the clear and unclear thoughts made me feel crazy. All the chaos and scrambled thinking is Satan's work. We have seen so far that God wants us peaceful, joyous, and feeling loved. He knows the importance of being healthy in your mind and emotions so the decisions you make are biblical and sound.

Give yourself a good shake and a talking-to when you are tempted to spend time hashing out all the old junk to God. It's a tug of war of sorts. Satan's choice of pain and drama versus God's comfort and tranquility. Give over your chaos to God. Ask him to clear away all that you needn't concern yourself with. By releasing all that scrambles your brain to God, you free yourself from the tug of war. You give all the power to God, leaving Satan without a say. It's just you and God planning, accessing, and choosing for you. God is tranquility, peace, and harmony. He longs for you to know that calm.

"Seek his will in all you do, and he will show you which path to take."

—Proverbs 3:6

PRAYER

Do I even have a mind to save, at this point? Sometimes I wonder. Satan is the master of confusion. If I am confused, have

I let Satan in, Lord? I curse Satan and insist he leave me, by the blood of your son, Jesus Christ. I do not want that vile thing disturbing my thoughts. Lord, restore my sound mind and cause me to turn my eyes only to you.

"Trust in the LORD *with all your heart; do not depend on your own understanding. Seek his will in all you do, and he will show you which path to take. . . . Joyful is the person who finds wisdom, the one who gains understanding. . . . My child, don't lose sight of common sense and discernment. Hang on to them."*

—Proverbs 3:5-6,13,21

"Doing wrong is fun for a fool, but living wisely brings pleasure to the sensible."

—Proverbs 10:23

"And now, dear brothers and sisters, one final thing. Fix your thoughts on what is true, and honorable, and right, and pure, and lovely, and admirable. Think about things that are excellent and worthy of praise. Keep putting into practice all you learned and received from me—everything you heard from me and saw me doing. Then the God of peace will be with you. . . . Not that I was ever in need, for I have learned how to be content with whatever I have. I know how to live on almost nothing or with everything. I have learned the secret of living in every situation, whether it is with a full stomach or empty, with plenty or little. For I can do everything through Christ, who gives me strength."

—Philippians 4:8-9,11-13

"So letting your sinful nature control your mind leads to death. But letting the Spirit control your mind leads to life and peace."

—Romans 8:6

"For God has not given us a spirit of fear and timidity, but of power, love, and self-discipline."

—2 Timothy 1:7

"We destroy every proud obstacle that keeps people from knowing God. We capture their rebellious thoughts and teach them to obey Christ."

—2 Corinthians 10:5

"Rejoice in our confident hope. Be patient in trouble, and keep on praying."

—Romans 12:12

"For, 'Who can know the Lord's thoughts? Who knows enough to teach him?' But we understand these things, for we have the mind of Christ."

—1 Corinthians 2:16

"Instead, let the Spirit renew your thoughts and attitudes."

—Ephesians 4:23

"You must have the same attitude that Christ Jesus had."

—Philippians 2:5

"But you should keep a clear mind in every situation. Don't be afraid of suffering for the Lord. Work at telling others the Good News, and fully carry out the ministry God has given you."

—2 Timothy 4:5

"Think about the things of heaven, not the things of earth."

—Colossians 3:2

"You will keep in perfect peace all who trust in you, all whose thoughts are fixed on you!"

—Isaiah 26:3

"Give all your worries and cares to God, for he cares about you."

—1 Peter 5:7

"And you will know the truth, and the truth will set you free."

—John 8:32

"Doing wrong is fun for a fool, but living wisely brings pleasure to the sensible."

—Proverbs 10:23

"Remember your leaders who taught you the word of God. Think of all the good that has come from their lives, and follow the example of their faith."

—Hebrews 13:7

"So think clearly and exercise self-control. Look forward to the gracious salvation that will come to you when Jesus Christ is revealed to the world."

—1 Peter 1:13

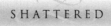

ASK GOD TO UNJUMBLE YOUR THOUGHTS. HE IS CLARITY.

WALK ALONG THE WATER'S EDGE.

SPIRITUAL HELP

The value of a strong spiritual network cannot be overstated. A strong network is a powerful tool when you haven't the strength or the resolve to deal with the onslaught of emotional arrows fired at you.

All the circumstances of this trying time erode the spirit. You might find your faith on shaky ground. Your willingness to "let go and let God" may be wavering. Your inability to fight temptation may have hit an all-time high. Your spiritual network doesn't take your burden from you, but your network shoulders some of the weight. They comfort, guide, and assist you. Surrounding yourself with other believers, your pastor, and godly councilors will serve to keep you focused and keep your eyes on God. You don't want to miss what he has for you.

"The godly offer good council, they teach right from wrong."

—Psalm 37:30

PRAYER

I need all the help I can get right now. My greatest lack is in the matters of the spirit. Surround me with spirit-filled people, Lord. Because this is my area of greatest lack, it is also the area I can grow in the greatest amount. I am excited to know you better.

"If I were you, I would go to God and present my case to him. He does great things too marvelous to understand. He performs countless miracles."

—Job 5:8-9

"Teach me to do your will, for you are my God. May your gracious Spirit lead me forward on a firm footing."

—Psalm 143:10

"Your own ears will hear him. Right behind you a voice will say, 'This is the way you should go,' whether to the right or to the left."

—Isaiah 30:21

"Jesus spoke to the people once more and said, 'I am the light of the world. If you follow me, you won't have to walk in darkness, because you will have the light that leads to life.' . . . Jesus said to the people who believed in him, 'You are truly my disciples if you remain faithful to my teachings. And you will know the truth, and the truth will set you free.'"

—John 8:12,31-32

"A final word: Be strong in the Lord and in his mighty power. Put on all of God's armor so that you will be able to stand firm against all strategies of the devil."

—Ephesians 6:10-11

"So let us come boldly to the throne of our gracious God. There we will receive his mercy, and we will find grace to help us when we need it most."

—Hebrews 4:16

"So be strong and courageous, all you who put your hope in the LORD*!"*

—Psalm 31:24

"So we can say with confidence, 'The Lord is my helper, so I will have no fear. What can mere people do to me?'"

—Hebrews 13:6

"The LORD *is my strength and shield. I trust him with all my heart. He helps me, and my heart is filled with joy. I burst out in songs of thanksgiving."*

—Psalm 28:7

"Unless the LORD *had helped me, I would soon have settled in the silence of the grave."*

—Psalm 94:17

"But you, dear friends, must build each other up in your most holy faith, pray in the power of the Holy Spirit."

—Jude 1:20

"The LORD *says, 'I will guide you along the best pathway for your life. I will advise you and watch over you.'"*

—Psalm 32:8

"For I hold you by your right hand—I, the LORD *your God. And I say to you, 'Don't be afraid. I am here to help you.'"*

—Isaiah 41:13

"So don't go to war without wise guidance; victory depends on having many advisers."

—Proverbs 24:6

"My help comes from the LORD*, who made heaven and earth!"*

—Psalm 121:2

"He replied, 'What is impossible for people is possible with God.'"

—Luke 18:27

"He will rescue the poor when they cry to him; he will help the oppressed, who have no one to defend them."

—Psalm 72:12

"Confess your sins to each other and pray for each other so that you may be healed. The earnest prayer of a righteous person has great power and produces wonderful results."

—James 5:16

"Give all your worries and cares to God, for he cares about you."

—1 Peter 5:7

"O Israel, trust the LORD*! He is your helper and your shield."*

—Psalm 115:9

"Then the Levites from the clans of Kohath and Korah stood to praise the LORD*, the God of Israel, with a very loud shout."*

—2 Chronicles 20:19

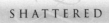

PLACE YOURSELF IN THE CENTER OF BELIEVERS AND DRAW STRENGTH FROM THEM.

SEND A THANK YOU NOTE TO THE CHURCH SECRETARY.

TEMPTATION

God knows our weaknesses and what roll temptation plays. But he does not tempt us. That is Satan's business. Satan loves the process of temptation. When we stumble, Satan relishes it. I was tempted on every front. I struggled against that temptation. When I won the fight, I felt master of my life. When I failed, I felt like I had been mastered.

Temptation is at every turn in life. You can't outrun it. Satan can keep up his relentless pursuit. He makes it a daily challenge for you. He knows your weaknesses. He knows how to cause you to fail. He gets more and more clever at finding the devices that will ensure his dominance over you. Your best defense is arming yourself with scripture. Throw a zinger at Satan, and watch him slink back into the darkness. Why not ask God to shield you when temptation presents itself? He yearns to hear from you and arm you against Satan's ways.

"But the Lord is faithful; he will strengthen you and guard you from the evil one."

—2 Thessalonians 3:3

PRAYER

Holy cow, this is huge, Lord. I am single now and the temptations are enormous and plentiful. There is no mystery to fighting temptation, initially. I simply have to keep my distance from where the temptation is. But if I find myself in a situation, Lord, I know you have a way out for me if I seek you. Lord, do not leave me now.

"People with integrity walk safely, but those who follow crooked paths will slip and fall."

—Proverbs 10:9

"The temptations in your life are no different from what others experience. And God is faithful. He will not allow the temptation to be more than you can stand. When you are tempted, he will show you a way out so that you can endure."

—1 Corinthians 10:13

"So I say, let the Holy Spirit guide your lives. Then you won't be doing what your sinful nature craves."

—Galatians 5:16

"Therefore, since we are surrounded by such a huge crowd of witnesses to the life of faith, let us strip off every weight that slows us down, especially the sin that so easily trips us up."

—Hebrews 12:1

"So get rid of all the filth and evil in your lives, and humbly accept the word God has planted in your hearts, for it has the power to save your souls."

—James 1:21

"So put to death the sinful, earthly things lurking within you. Have nothing to do with sexual immorality, impurity, lust, and evil desires. Don't be greedy, for a greedy person is an idolater, worshiping the things of this world."

—Colossians 3:5

"A final word: Be strong in the Lord and in his mighty power. Put on all of God's armor so that you will be able to stand firm against all strategies of the devil."

—Ephesians 6:10-11

"Since he himself has gone through suffering and testing, he is able to help us when we are being tested."

—Hebrews 2:18

"This High Priest of ours understands our weaknesses, for he faced all of the same testings we do, yet he did not sin. So let us come boldly to the throne of our gracious God. There we will receive his mercy, and we will find grace to help us when we need it most."

—Hebrews 4:15-16

"So you see, the Lord knows how to rescue godly people from their trials, even while keeping the wicked under punishment until the day of final judgment."

—2 Peter 2:9

"So be careful how you live. Don't live like fools, but like those who are wise."

—Ephesians 5:15

"Stay alert! Watch out for your great enemy, the devil. He prowls around like a roaring lion, looking for someone to devour."

—1 Peter 5:8

"So humble yourselves before God. Resist the devil, and he will flee from you."

—James 4:7

"You must not follow the crowd in doing wrong. When you are called to testify in a dispute, do not be swayed by the crowd to twist justice."

—Exodus 23:2

"My child, if sinners entice you, turn your back on them!"

—Proverbs 1:10

"Don't do as the wicked do, and don't follow the path of evildoers. Don't even think about it; don't go that way. Turn away and keep moving."

—Proverbs 4:14-15

"Keep watch and pray, so that you will not give in to temptation. For the spirit is willing, but the body is weak."

—Mark 14:38

"But because you are stubborn and refuse to turn from your sin, you are storing up terrible punishment for yourself. For a day of anger is coming, when God's righteous judgment will be revealed."

—Romans 2:5

"Run from anything that stimulates youthful lusts. Instead, pursue righteous living, faithfulness, love, and peace. Enjoy the companionship of those who call on the Lord with pure hearts. Again I say, don't get involved in foolish, ignorant arguments that only start fights."

—2 Timothy 2:22-23

FIGHT THOSE INEVITABLE TEMPTATIONS. GIVING IN WILL DELAY WHAT GOD HAS FOR YOU.

LISTEN TO A PREACHER'S SERMON.

TROUBLES

Troubles are the actual things, events, and circumstances that we worry about or fear. They are the experiences of today that we couldn't or didn't plan for yesterday and cannot necessarily remedy for ourselves tomorrow. We all have them. We all know what they are. And it doesn't matter if we are in the throes of a divorce or not. Life means trials, tests, and troubles. God tells us many times throughout scripture to bring our troubles to him. He offers to be our salvation, our strength, our fortress, our rescuer, our rock, and our hiding place. God's power knows no limits.

> *"I cried out to the Lord in my great trouble, and he answered me."*
>
> —Jonah 2:1

PRAYER

My troubles are so many that I am overwhelmed. Lord, I know you are in control and working on all my troubles. Please remind me often that all I have to do is trust you to guide me through the troubled times.

"He comforts us in all our troubles so that we can comfort others. When they are troubled, we will be able to give them the same comfort God has given us."

—2 Corinthians 1:4

"Bend down, O Lord, *and hear my prayer; answer me, for I need your help."*

—Psalm 86:1

"For our present troubles are small and won't last very long. Yet they produce for us a glory that vastly outweighs them and will last forever!"

—2 Corinthians 4:17

"The Lord *is good, a strong refuge when trouble comes. He is close to those who trust in him."*

—Nahum 1:7

"Your promise revives me; it comforts me in all my troubles."

—Psalm 119:50

"Are any of you suffering hardships? You should pray. Are any of you happy? You should sing praises."

—James 5:13

"In times of trouble, may the Lord *answer your cry. May the name of the God of Jacob keep you safe from all harm."*

—Psalm 20:1

"Though I am surrounded by troubles, you will protect me from the anger of my enemies. You reach out your hand, and the power of your right hand saves me."

—Psalm 138:7

"The righteous person faces many troubles, but the LORD comes to the rescue each time."

—Psalm 34:19

"Then call on me when you are in trouble, and I will rescue you, and you will give me glory."

—Psalm 50:15

"God is our refuge and strength, always ready to help in times of trouble."

—Psalm 46:1

"For you are my hiding place; you protect me from trouble. You surround me with songs of victory."

—Psalm 32:7

"I took my troubles to the LORD; I cried out to him, and he answered my prayer."

—Psalm 120:1

"The LORD rescues the godly; he is their fortress in times of trouble."

—Psalm 37:39

"You cried to me in trouble, and I saved you; I answered out of the thundercloud and tested your faith when there was no water at Meribah."

—Psalm 81:7

"I will call to you whenever I'm in trouble, and you will answer me."

—Psalm 86:7

"Give your burdens to the LORD, and he will take care of you. He will not permit the godly to slip and fall."

—Psalm 55:22

"When they call on me, I will answer; I will be with them in trouble. I will rescue and honor them."

—Psalm 91:15

"Come back to the place of safety, all you prisoners who still have hope! I promise this very day that I will repay two blessings for each of your troubles."

—Zechariah 9:12

"You have allowed me to suffer much hardship, but you will restore me to life again and lift me up from the depths of the earth."

—Psalm 71:20

"So you handed them over to their enemies, who made them suffer. But in their time of trouble they cried to you, and you heard them from heaven. In your great mercy, you sent them liberators who rescued them from their enemies."

—Nehemiah 9:27

"O LORD*, you are my lamp. The* LORD *lights up my darkness."*

—2 Samuel 22:29

"Those who obey him will not be punished. Those who are wise will find a time and a way to do what is right, for there is a time and a way for everything, even when a person is in trouble."

—Ecclesiastes 8:5-6

GOD WANTS YOU TO UNLOAD YOUR TROUBLES ON HIM. THEN JUST RELAX AND WATCH HIM WORK.

TAKE DONUTS TO WORK.

TRUST

I will never trust anyone, especially a man, ever again! I probably shouted this vow a couple hundred times in the year of my divorce proceedings. I knew I couldn't trust my ex. I didn't know if I could trust my lawyer. I didn't trust the laws of my state. And I wasn't sure about my auto mechanic—or my plumber.

Basically I had no one I felt sure about. I was challenged to put my trust in people, to meet the needs in all areas of my life. I didn't know I only had to trust in God. There are so many people in God's army that can be of help to you, but it will mean you have to step out in faith. Take care not to label everyone as being untrustworthy. It is hard to trust again, but you can do this. Step by step, day by day, God will help you find the sincere and honest ones. With each properly placed trust, your faith in people will be restored.

"O Lord, I give my life to you. I trust in you, my God!"

—Psalm 25:1 2

PRAYER

You know I have trust issues, Lord. Can you blame me? I understand that I need trust, but Lord, I live in the world. How do I get by, when I feel I can't trust the people I have to rely on in the physical world? How does trusting you translate to my everyday life? Help me understand.

"He has given me a new song to sing, a hymn of praise to our God. Many will see what he has done and be amazed. They will put their trust in the Lord. Oh, the joys of those who trust the Lord, who have no confidence in the proud or in those who worship idols."

—Psalm 40:3-4

"They do not fear bad news; they confidently trust the Lord *to care for them."*

—Psalm 112:7

"If I were you, I would go to God and present my case to him. He does great things too marvelous to understand. He performs countless miracles."

—Job 5:8-9

"O my people, trust in him at all times. Pour out your heart to him, for God is our refuge."

—Psalm 62:8

"Those who know your name trust in you, for you, O Lord*, do not abandon those who search for you."*

—Psalm 9:10

"We put our hope in the Lord*. He is our help and our shield. In him our hearts rejoice, for we trust in his holy name."*

—Psalm 33:20-21

"Those who listen to instruction will prosper; those who trust the Lord *will be joyful."*

—Proverbs 16:20

"Commit everything you do to the Lord*. Trust him, and he will help you. He will make your innocence radiate like the dawn, and the justice of your cause will shine like the noonday sun."*

—Psalm 37:5-6

"But blessed are those who trust in the LORD and have made the LORD their hope and confidence."

—Jeremiah 17:7

"This I declare about the LORD: He alone is my refuge, my place of safety; he is my God, and I trust him."

—Psalm 91:2

"Trust in the LORD with all your heart; do not depend on your own understanding."

—Proverbs 3:5

"The LORD is good to those who depend on him, to those who search for him."

—Lamentations 3:25

"God will do this, for he is faithful to do what he says, and he has invited you into partnership with his Son, Jesus Christ our Lord."

—1 Corinthians 1:9

"So do not throw away this confident trust in the Lord. Remember the great reward it brings you!"

—Hebrews 10:35

"I have come as a light to shine in this dark world, so that all who put their trust in me will no longer remain in the dark."

—John 12:46

"I am worn out waiting for your rescue, but I have put my hope in your word."

—Psalm 119:81

"Make them holy by your truth; teach them your word, which is truth."

—John 17:17

"O LORD of Heaven's Armies, what joy for those who trust in you."

—Psalm 84:12

"God's way is perfect. All the LORD's promises prove true. He is a shield for all who look to him for protection."

—2 Samuel 22:31

"I am teaching you today—yes, you—so you will trust in the LORD."

—Proverbs 22:19

"O LORD, I give my life to you. I trust in you, my God! Do not let me be disgraced, or let my enemies rejoice in my defeat. No one who trusts in you will ever be disgraced, but disgrace comes to those who try to deceive others."

—Psalm 25:1-3

THE LORD WILL INCREASE YOUR FAITH SO YOU WILL LEARN TO TRUST HIM.

INVITE A FRIEND TO DINNER.

VENGEANCE

This is a feeling I laid claim to in an enormous way. Of all the feelings I felt, getting even was huge. Truth be known, I relished the pleasure I would feel plunging a kitchen knife into my ex's black heart. Thank goodness God understands our human longing to make the creep pay. Even my dearest friend hinted she would help clean up the mess and dump the body.

I am being dramatic here. Don't beat yourself up if something like this occurred to you. But I'd like to suggest you find your knees, quick. Pray for strength to take your hands off this one. I expect vengeance might feel pretty good for about three minutes, then you can add it to the pile of things you need to seek forgiveness for. It is a powerful desire to make the guilty pay for the hurt that they did to you. But consider, who can do a better job of vengeance than God?

> *"Don't say, 'I will get even for this wrong.' Wait for the Lord to handle the matter."*
>
> —Proverbs 20:22

PRAYER

Lord, you know I ache for vengeance and I know I need to leave it up to you. I pray that you take this feeling from me. Help me to replace the desire for vengeance with the desire to forgive. Remind me often that the desire for vengeance is a waste of my time, energy, and peace. Remind me often, Lord, that you have this one.

"The Lord himself will fight for you. Just stay calm."

—Exodus 14:14

"He said, 'Listen, all you people of Judah and Jerusalem! Listen, King Jehoshaphat! This is what the LORD *says: Do not be afraid! Don't be discouraged by this mighty army, for the battle is not yours, but God's. . . . But you will not even need to fight. Take your positions; then stand still and watch the Lord's victory.'"*

—2 Chronicles 20:17

"The Lord frustrates the plans of the nations and thwarts all their schemes."

—Psalm 33:10

"God has spoken plainly, and I have heard it many times: Power, O God, belongs to you; unfailing love, O Lord, is yours. Surely you repay all people according to what they have done."

—Psalm 62:11-12

"What blessings await you when people hate you and exclude you and mock you and curse you as evil because you follow the Son of Man."

—Luke 6:22

"You intended to harm me, but God intended it all for good. He brought me to this position so I could save the lives of many people."

—Genesis 50:20

"But in that coming day no weapon turned against you will succeed. You will silence every voice raised up to accuse you. These benefits are enjoyed by the servants of the LORD*; their vindication will come from me. I, the* LORD*, have spoken!"*

—Isaiah 54:17

"Say to those with fearful hearts, 'Be strong, and do not fear, for your God is coming to destroy your enemies. He is coming to save you.'"

—Isaiah 35:4

"I will execute terrible vengeance against them to punish them for what they have done. And when I have inflicted my revenge, they will know that I am the LORD.*"*

—Ezekiel 25:17

"The godly will rejoice when they see injustice avenged. They will wash their feet in the blood of the wicked. Then at last everyone will say, 'There truly is a reward for those who live for God; surely there is a God who judges justly here on earth.'"

—Psalm 58:10-11

"But Jesus answered by saying to them, 'You don't know what you are asking! Are you able to drink from the bitter cup of suffering I am about to drink?' 'Oh yes,' they replied, 'we are able!'"

—Matthew 20:22

"O LORD*, the God of vengeance, O God of vengeance, let your glorious justice shine forth!"*

—Psalm 94:1

"The Egyptians will lose heart, and I will confuse their plans. They will plead with their idols for wisdom and call on spirits, mediums, and those who consult the spirits of the dead."

—Isaiah 19:3

"Never pay back evil with more evil. Do things in such a way that everyone can see you are honorable. . . . Dear friends, never take revenge. Leave that to the righteous anger of God. For the Scriptures say, 'I will take revenge; I will pay them back,' says the Lord."

—Romans 12:17,19

"But their evil intentions will be exposed when the light shines on them."

—Ephesians 5:13

"I trust in you, my God! Do not let me be disgraced, or let my enemies rejoice in my defeat."

—Psalm 25:2

"The Lord *protects the foreigners among us. He cares for the orphans and widows, but he frustrates the plans of the wicked."*

—Psalm 146:9

KILL EM' WITH KINDNESS AND PRAYER.

ICE CREAM IS SWEETER THAN VENGENACE.

VICTORY

Oh, sweet victory. Who doesn't understand the appeal of winning or being victorious? Unlike the victory we know in a sports arena, being victorious in Christ is not about beating your challenger. Spiritual victory is knowing who sits upon the throne, who has your back, who loves you beyond measure, who calms your fears, who knows your heart, and so has your victory as his plan for you. I pray you have the patience to spend time with God and his Word. The rewards will spell victory for you.

> *"I wait quietly before God, for my victory comes from him."*
>
> —Psalm 62:1

PRAYER

This is something I am really excited about. I never imagined I could have victory anywhere in my sorry little life. Victory sounds like an enormous task, but I trust you, Lord. You promise victory and I am claiming it.

"But Eleazar and David held their ground in the middle of the field and beat back the Philistines. So the Lord saved them by giving them a great victory."

—1 Chronicles 11:14

"'But for you who fear my name, the Sun of Righteousness will rise with healing in his wings. And you will go free, leaping with joy like calves let out to pasture. On the day when I act, you will tread upon the wicked as if they were dust under your feet,' says the Lord of Heaven's Armies."

—Malachi 4:2-3

"But thank God! He gives us victory over sin and death through our Lord Jesus Christ."

—1 Corinthians 15:57

"For every child of God defeats this evil world, and we achieve this victory through our faith."

—1 John 5:4

"Yes, the LORD *is for me; he will help me. I will look in triumph at those who hate me. . . . The* LORD *is my strength and my song; he has given me victory."*

—Psalm 118:7,14

"The LORD *is my strength and my song; he has given me victory. This is my God, and I will praise him—my father's God, and I will exalt him!"*

—Exodus 15:2

"I wait quietly before God, for my victory comes from him. . . . My victory and honor come from God alone. He is my refuge, a rock where no enemy can reach me."

—Psalm 62:1,7

"Sing a new song to the LORD, for he has done wonderful deeds. His right hand has won a mighty victory; his holy arm has shown his saving power!"

—Psalm 98:1

"For the LORD your God is going with you! He will fight for you against your enemies, and he will give you victory!"

—Deuteronomy 20:4

"So David triumphed over the Philistine with only a sling and a stone, for he had no sword."

—1 Samuel 17:50

"Yours, O LORD, is the greatness, the power, the glory, the victory, and the majesty. Everything in the heavens and on earth is yours, O LORD, and this is your kingdom. We adore you as the one who is over all things."

—1 Chronicles 29:11

"He will not crush the weakest reed or put out a flickering candle. Finally he will cause justice to be victorious."

—Matthew 12:20

"No, despite all these things, overwhelming victory is ours through Christ, who loved us."

—Romans 8:37

"Victory comes from you, O LORD. May you bless your people."

—Psalm 3:8

"But you belong to God, my dear children. You have already won a victory over those people, because the Spirit who lives in you is greater than the spirit who lives in the world."

—1 John 4:4

"Do not love this world nor the things it offers you, for when you love the world, you do not have the love of the Father in you."

—1 John 2:15

"In your strength I can crush an army; with my God I can scale any wall. . . . He trains my hands for battle; he strengthens my arm to draw a bronze bow. You have given me your shield of victory. Your right hand supports me; your help has made me great. You have made a wide path for my feet to keep them from slipping. . . . You have armed me with strength for the battle; you have subdued my enemies under my feet."

—Psalm 18:29,34-36,39

"For the LORD *delights in his people; he crowns the humble with victory."*

—Psalm 149:4

"But he himself will be refreshed from brooks along the way. He will be victorious."

—Psalm 110:7

"See, God has come to save me. I will trust in him and not be afraid. The LORD GOD *is my strength and my song; he has given me victory."*

—Isaiah 12:2

MIRACLES ARE HAPPENING RIGHT NOW. CLAIM ONE FOR YOURSELF.

TURN UP THE VOLUME ON A PRAISE AND WORSHIP CD.

WISDOM

Clearly, I lacked wisdom for most of my second marriage. Violations to our marriage were everywhere. I just didn't see the truth of the situation. All was fully revealed post-divorce. So I asked myself, "am I to be trusted to be wise now?" Of course, the answer to that question was, heck no.

Rest easy if you find yourself having the same thoughts. First of all, there is nothing wrong with making every effort to save your marriage. If turning a blind eye on suspicions was how you did it, how can anyone find fault with that? The decision to violate the marriage was not yours. That responsibility lies with your husband. So forgive yourself for what you are calling lack of wisdom. Wisdom is one thing God has handled. He is the Almighty, the Creator of Heaven and Earth. He made you. He has the wisdom you seek. So don't rely on your own understanding. Take your decisions to God in prayer.

"I will certainly give you the wisdom and knowledge you requested."
—2 Chronicles 1:12

PRAYER

Thank you, God, that I don't have to be wise all the time. I only have to pray for your wisdom to guide me. Right now I feel deceived, foolish, inept, and unprepared. Remind me, Lord, to put all matter before you, before I act.

"But there is a spirit within people, the breath of the Almighty within them, that makes them intelligent."

—Job 32:8

"How wonderful to be wise, to analyze and interpret things. Wisdom lights up a person's face, softening its harshness."

—Ecclesiastes 8:1

"God gives wisdom, knowledge, and joy to those who please him. But if a sinner becomes wealthy, God takes the wealth away and gives it to those who please him. This, too, is meaningless—like chasing the wind."

—Ecclesiastes 2:26

"The LORD *says, 'I will guide you along the best pathway for your life. I will advise you and watch over you.'"*

—Psalm 32:8

"For the LORD *grants wisdom! From his mouth come knowledge and understanding."*

—Proverbs 2:6

"Fools think their own way is right, but the wise listen to others."

—Proverbs 12:15

"How much better to get wisdom than gold, and good judgment than silver!"

—Proverbs 16:16

"A wise person is hungry for knowledge, while the fool feeds on trash."

—Proverbs 15:14

"Listen to his instructions, and store them in your heart."

—Job 22:22

"Fear of the Lord *is the foundation of true wisdom. All who obey his commandments will grow in wisdom."*

—Psalm 111:10

"He has showered his kindness on us, along with all wisdom and understanding."

—Ephesians 1:8

"I thank and praise you, God of my ancestors, for you have given me wisdom and strength. You have told me what we asked of you and revealed to us what the king demanded."

—Daniel 2:23

"Get wisdom; develop good judgment. Don't forget my words or turn away from them. . . . Getting wisdom is the wisest thing you can do! And whatever else you do, develop good judgment. If you prize wisdom, she will make you great. Embrace her, and she will honor you. . . . Take hold of my instructions; don't let them go. Guard them, for they are the key to life."

—Proverbs 4:5,7-8,13

"Your word is a lamp to guide my feet and a light for my path."

—Psalm 119:105

"Fear of the Lord is the foundation of wisdom. Knowledge of the Holy One results in good judgment. Wisdom will multiply your days and add years to your life."

—Proverbs 9:10-11

"Get the truth and never sell it; also get wisdom, discipline, and good judgment."

—Proverbs 23:23

"Wisdom and money can get you almost anything, but only wisdom can save your life."

—Ecclesiastes 7:12

"For my words are wise, and my thoughts are filled with insight."

—Psalm 49:3

"For I will give you the right words and such wisdom that none of your opponents will be able to reply or refute you!"

—Luke 21:15

"Study this Book of Instruction continually. Meditate on it day and night so you will be sure to obey everything written in it. Only then will you prosper and succeed in all you do."

—Joshua 1:8

"Get all the advice and instruction you can, so you will be wise the rest of your life."

—Proverbs 19:20

"O my people, listen to my instructions. Open your ears to what I am saying."

—Psalm 78:1

*YOU CAN RELAX,
GOD'S GOT THIS.
JUST LOOK TO
HIS WORD.*

SAY JESUS' NAME TEN TIMES. POWERFUL!

WORRY

In the grand scheme of things, we are small and ill-equipped to handle many of our worrisome matters. If making adjustments, careful planning, or more money aren't suitable answers, then we feel we are defenseless. That is an overwhelming idea! But therein lies the basis of worry and the flaw in our thinking.

Worry is without power. Worrying more doesn't yield more results. God commands us to worry about nothing and pray about everything. Imagine the peace and freedom you would enjoy if you really understood that you never have to worry again.

"Give your burdens to the Lord, and he will take care of you."
—Psalm 55:22

PRAYER

I am sick to death with all this worry. It is stealing my joy. I want my joy back. I can hardly remember a time when I wasn't worried. But I look back at old pictures and see the happiness I used to feel. Lord, take this worry from me. Teach me to rely on you. Let me feel your peace. Take the worry from my face and let your light shine instead.

"Don't worry about the wicked or envy those who do wrong."

—Psalm 37:1

"Worry weighs a person down; an encouraging word cheers a person up."

—Proverbs 12:25

"And why worry about a speck in your friend's eye when you have a log in your own?"

—Luke 6:41

"Don't worry about anything; instead, pray about everything. Tell God what you need, and thank him for all he has done. Then you will experience God's peace, which exceeds anything we can understand. His peace will guard your hearts and minds as you live in Christ Jesus."

—Philippians 4:6-7

"So be strong and courageous! Do not be afraid and do not panic before them. For the LORD *your God will personally go ahead of you. He will neither fail you nor abandon you."*

—Deuteronomy 31:6

"Search me, O God, and know my heart; test me and know my anxious thoughts. Point out anything in me that offends you, and lead me along the path of everlasting life."

—Psalm 139:23-24

"Can all your worries add a single moment to your life? . . . So don't worry about tomorrow, for tomorrow will bring its own worries. Today's trouble is enough for today."

—Matthew 6:27,34

"Give all your worries and cares to God, for he cares about you."

—1 Peter 5:7

"For nothing is impossible with God."

—Luke 1:37

"And when you are brought to trial in the synagogues and before rulers and authorities, don't worry about how to defend yourself or what to say, for the Holy Spirit will teach you at that time what needs to be said. . . . That is why I tell you not to worry about everyday life—whether you have enough food to eat or enough clothes to wear."

—Luke 12:11-12,22

"They are like trees planted along a riverbank, with roots that reach deep into the water. Such trees are not bothered by the heat or worried by long months of drought. Their leaves stay green, and they never stop producing fruit."

—Jeremiah 17:8

"Then Jesus said, 'Come to me, all of you who are weary and carry heavy burdens, and I will give you rest.'"

—Matthew 11:28

"Watch out! Don't let your hearts be dulled by carousing and drunkenness, and by the worries of this life."

—Luke 21:34

"And we know that God causes everything to work together for the good of those who love God and are called according to his purpose for them."

—Romans 8:28

"I see that the Lord is always with me. I will not be shaken, for he is right beside me."

—Acts 2:25

"Now I want you to know, dear brothers and sisters, what God in his kindness has done through the churches in Macedonia. They

are being tested by many troubles, and they are very poor. But they are also filled with abundant joy, which has overflowed in rich generosity."

—2 Corinthians 8:1-2

GOD SUPPLIES ALL YOUR NEEDS.

WORRY ABOUT NOTHING. PRAY ABOUT EVERYTHING.

SOME FINAL THOUGHTS

You have been on a roller-coaster of emotions. When you began your healing, you also began a spiritual journey that we hope continues for the whole remainder of your life. We hope you found value in what our experiences have taught us. We know that women, including ourselves, are capable of extraordinary bravery and feats of heroism. But when it comes to an unwanted divorce or the death of the man we love, we can find ourselves crippled by a sense of loss and the crush of conflicting emotions. The fear and uncertainty can make life unbearable.

Our motive, first and foremost, was to commiserate with you. We wanted to express our love for you and our grief at what you are going through. We wanted to love you through it. We hope you are standing a bit taller. We hope you have forgiveness in your heart for all the players in your own painful drama. We hope the joy has returned to your countenance and the smile has returned to your face.

As you go forward with your life, we pray God lights your path. We pray God will show you your purpose and how to fulfill it. We pray you never betray who God meant for you to be. And lastly, we pray that no man will ever cost you your peace again.

We are happy for you and rejoice in the life that is ahead of you.

Blessings and love,

Sharon and Dyann

ABOUT THE AUTHORS

Sharon Steinman lives in Lake Charles, Louisiana. She has three wonderful children and three great "in-loves," who have given her the best gifts—her seven grandchildren. Sharon enjoys traveling, cooking, crafts, and loves to be outdoors. She is happy to share her testimony and the joy of the Lord wherever she goes.

Dyann Munoz hails from Detroit, Michigan, but now calls Mobile, Alabama home. She is a proud mom of two amazing sons and their lovely wives. She has four grandchildren that are the sugary-goodness in her life. When Dyann isn't working as a designer or writing, she loves to cook, sew, read, and paint.

If this book has touched your life,
the authors would love to hear from you.
You can contact them directly at twogoodhearts@gmail.com
or visit their website at twogoodhearts.net.